ENGAGING INTERNATIONAL ALUMNI
AS STRATEGIC PARTNERS

ENGAGING INTERNATIONAL ALUMNI
AS STRATEGIC PARTNERS

BY SANDRA RINCÓN, MSc, AND GRETCHEN DOBSON, EdD

Engaging International Alumni as Strategic Partners

By Sandra Rincón and Gretchen Dobson

NAFSA: Association of International Educators
1425 K Street, NW
12th Floor
Washington, DC 20005

NAFSA is the largest and most comprehensive association of professionals committed to advancing international higher education. Based in the United States, we provide programs, products, services, and a physical and virtual meeting space for the worldwide community of international educators. The association provides leadership to its varied constituencies through establishing principles of good practice and providing professional development opportunities. NAFSA encourages networking among professionals, convenes conferences and collaborative dialogues, and promotes research and knowledge creation to strengthen and serve the field. We lead the way in advocating for a better world through international education.

Library of Congress Control Number: 2020953039
ISBN: 978-1-942719-41-0 (Print)

Edited by Dara Liling
Design and Layout by Dion Faradonez

Copyright © 2021 by NAFSA: Association of International Educators. No part of this publication may be reproduced, stored in a retrieval system, or transmitted in any form or by any means, electronic, mechanical, photocopying, recording, scanning, or otherwise, except as permitted under Section 107 or 108 of the United States Copyright Act, without the prior written permission of the publisher. Requests to the publisher for permission should be addressed to Publications@nafsa.org.
Printed in the United States.

BULK PURCHASES

Quantity discounts are available for workshops and staff development. Call 1.866.538.1927 to order.

First edition, 2021
10 9 8 7 6 5 4 3 2

Contents

Dedications vii
Acknowledgments ix
Foreword | Jeffrey M. Riedinger, PhD xiii

Introduction 1

CHAPTER 1
Why Higher Education Should Engage International Alumni 9

CHAPTER 2
International Alumni Relations Program Development 21

CHAPTER 3
A Framework for Growing and Maintaining International Alumni Engagement 41

CHAPTER 4
International Alumni Ambassador Programs 61

CHAPTER 5
Transformational Philanthropy: Alumni Giving to Advance the International Agenda | Maria Gallo, EdD, and Kevin Fleming, PhD 73

CHAPTER 6
The Roles of International Alumni: Perspectives from the Field .. 91
Brand and Reputation Management 94
Attracting and Retaining Talent 113
Employability for the Twenty-First Century 135
Innovation and Social Responsibility 154

Conclusion: A World of Help 175

About the Authors and Contributors 179

A Note on Process 185

Dedications

From Sandra

Engaging with international students and alumni has been and continues to be fulfilling and inspirational to me. I dedicate this book to Paul Scherrenberg, my husband, who has always supported me and enticed me to follow my heart. Whenever possible, he has joined me for the international visits, alumni events, conferences, and other learning opportunities I've had throughout my long career. He's been my wonderful life coach whose love and optimism has given me the impetus to overcome many challenges and enjoy whatever I do. Thank you for your infinite encouragement and patience!

From Gretchen

When I was a child, I combed through my parents' high school and college yearbooks, mesmerized by black and white photos of graduates, social functions, and sporting events, and of course, the notes that classmates penned in the margins next to their favorite photos. My late father, Al, was a devoted alum and volunteer leader of his high school and college classes. He remained loyal to his St. Mary's Gaels for more than 60 years and enjoyed sharing his alum life (and many rugby and basketball games) with his family and friends. My mother, Marilyn, also felt lifelong affinity and friendship with her Black Masque Honor Society sisters from San Jose State University, committing to annual reunions and traveling across state lines to be there on those special weekends. Together, my parents' active alumni lifestyles created an early awareness of how alumni relations can enrich a life; both instilled an interest in becoming active in alumni associations—and I certainly have done so. I dedicate this book to both of my parents for this formative gift of awareness and for their never-ending support for my chosen career.

I also dedicate this book to my husband, Michael, for accepting that nontraditional work hours and international travel have been part of the journey and for continuing to support each venture, such as this book, and its demands. I'm now home more than ever, Michael, and I'm so grateful for your love and friendship.

Acknowledgments

This book has been a community effort. We believe the collaborative nature of our research, interviews, and writing helped us produce our best effort. First and foremost, we thank the NAFSA team, led by Dara Liling, senior editor. We greatly appreciate Dara's enthusiasm for our subject, objective inquiries, clear editing, and never-ending flexibility. We also thank Wendy Rubin, Dale LaFleur, and Joann Ng Hartmann for lending their encouragement, support, and guidance from start to finish.

We are indebted to Maria Gallo and Kevin Fleming for contributing an entire chapter. We greatly appreciate the ease of working together, their deep knowledge on the subject, and their generosity of making the time in such a tumultuous year. We know readers will benefit from and be inspired by their ability to convey strong, transformational examples of international alumni engagement.

Additionally, we want to thank our illustrious contributors who shared their case studies. We urge readers to learn more about this talented pool of professionals by turning to their biographies (starting on page 180).

And to the many colleagues across the world who created space for us to conduct interviews and multiple conversations in order to share their best practices in international alumni engagement—we thank you!

From Sandra

I'd also like to thank my community of exceptional women from whom I have been so fortunate to learn so much and with whom I continue to share many discussions on the fascinating world of international alumni relations. They have helped me clarify my ideas and assumptions and have provided me with countless insights and opportunities. Anne-Françoise Rutkowski has guided my academic and research endeavors on international higher education throughout the years. Nicole Fouchier opened the door to the enriching work of alumni relations. We have shared so many day-to-day lessons and countless laughs while working together. Dorothea Antonio encouraged me to share what I was developing on international alumni relations with others in NAFSA preconference workshops. Much of the LEARN Model of International Alumni Relations described in this book has been improved over the course of these workshops. Melanie Agnew, who always makes time for me no matter what, has shared deep knowledge on international education as organizational change that has been tremendously valuable, and she always challenges me to take my work a level deeper. Raphaela Kühn invited me to join her team in the inspirational EU ALUMNI project, and we've created many exciting events together. María Lucía Bermúdez Oviedo, whose energy moves mountains, has shown me how to navigate engagement in the virtual world. Roxana Fernández, whose serenity and company during what seemed like endless days of writing kept me focused, shared numerous insights as an international alum. And of course, thanks to Gretchen Dobson for being an open-minded and flexible writing partner, making time at odd hours in Australia so we could discuss the book, and sharing fun ideas on engagement. She's always ready for action to make the next thing happen.

Last but not least, I'd like to thank the many international alumni whom I have had the pleasure of getting to know well. I could fill constellations with their names, home countries, and generosity. Also, a very special thanks to my Colombian, American, and Dutch family for their love. They have encouraged my passion for helping build communities to promote diversity for a more inclusive and kinder world. Thank you for being part of my journey.

From Gretchen

Additional words of gratitude to the University at Albany's School of Education's International Education Management and Leadership program for championing the topic of global alumni relations and providing me a platform for sharing my favorite topic with graduate students and higher education professionals from around the world. My affiliation with the program's leadership, fellow faculty, involved students, and invested alumni strengthen my interest in new forms of teaching and learning. And thanks to my writing partner, Sandra Rincón, whose care and attention to detail throughout each stage of the writing process and keen and inclusive sense of content and style created a tremendous learning opportunity for me from Day 1.

Foreword
By Jeffrey M. Riedinger, PhD

The phenomenon of international student mobility is not new to tertiary education. Many leading universities around the world can date the arrival of their first international students back more than a century and, in some instances, much further back than that. What is relatively new, however, is the dramatic increase in the scale and scope of international student mobility. The Organisation for Economic Co-operation and Development (OECD) estimates that international student mobility increased from roughly 800,000 students in 1975 to 1.3 million students in 1990 (ICEF Monitor 2017). By 2000, that figure was approximately 2.3 million, by 2010 it was more than 3.5 million, and by 2018 the total was 5.6 million (OECD 2020). The composition of international student mobility has also changed, both in terms of countries of origin and in the increasing mix of undergraduate students relative to graduate and professional students. These increases in the scale and composition of international student mobility create new challenges and opportunities for tertiary institutions as they work to better serve their international alumni and engage them in advancing comprehensive internationalization.

The nature of tertiary education and the student experience is also changing, as learners increasingly shift from solely participating in a few years of in-person undergraduate, professional, or graduate degree instruction to turning throughout their careers to their alma maters for upskilling and associated badges, certificates, and other credentials. This new generation of international alumni expects access to lifelong education and degree opportunities, just as current international students expect a more holistic array of services during their time on campus in support of their efforts to secure postgraduation employment and in their roles as international alumni. In turn, institutions have more opportunities to meaningfully engage international alumni in mutually beneficial ways throughout their careers and life cycles.

Although there were notable exceptions, particularly among elite institutions, for too long, too many tertiary institutions all but ignored their international alumni. Perhaps there was someone in alumni services who dedicated part of her or his time to welcoming international alumni when they returned to visit campus, but relatively few institutions had programs of, or processes for, ongoing and intentional engagement of international alumni. The relative inattention to international alumni in earlier years often reflected a mix of uncertainty about how to proceed, a dearth of experienced international alumni professionals, a lack of resources allotted to such initiatives, and a degree of skepticism about the prospects for philanthropic giving from international alumni, particularly graduate alumni.

As international student populations grew and institutions began to seek out their alumni around the world, institutions learned that there were countries with critical masses of international alumni who had established local alumni chapters decades ago. Consistent with the then-prevailing profile of international students, these chapters often reflected the work of graduate and professional alumni. They had the organizational experience and resources to operate such alumni chapters with little or no support from their alma mater. Although these autonomous chapters may have served their local alumni well, they were often disconnected from their alma mater and, equally significant, from international alumni chapters in other countries. In turn, they missed out on opportunities for collaboration, alignment of efforts, and cross-learning.

In recent decades, institutions have begun to see the opportunity and need to engage such alumni more intentionally and strategically. Some of the leading alumni services and international education professionals began to understand the opportunity for a more holistic engagement of international alumni. Faculty have built cross-national research collaborations with their former international students. Admissions offices increasingly look to international alumni to assist with international student recruitment. International offices connect study abroad programs and students to international alumni in relevant countries. Internship offices seek international alumni who can provide hands-on professional learning opportunities for domestic and international students alike. Career services offices connect with international alumni who can offer students career advice and employment opportunities.

In response to these trends, NAFSA is pleased to publish *Engaging International Alumni as Strategic Partners*, its first book on international alumni engagement to advance comprehensive internationalization. NAFSA has a long and proud history of engaging international students and promoting comprehensive internationalization and, therefore, was thrilled when two of the leading figures in the field of international alumni engagement submitted a proposal to put such a book together. The result is a timely and much-needed resource. In the pages that follow, Sandra Rincón, MSc, and Gretchen Dobson, EdD, take readers on a tour-de-force examination of international alumni engagement to further comprehensive internationalization. Their insights from first-hand experience are richly complemented by case studies provided by colleagues from around the world.

In this book, Rincón and Dobson offer compelling answers to the following questions:

- Why should institutions be more strategic and intentional in their engagement of international alumni?
- How can institutions develop, grow, and sustain effective programs of engagement?
- Where might such engagement begin and extend over time?
- What elements should such programs include, and what are their advantages?
- What is the potential impact of such engagement in philanthropic terms as well as for brand and reputation management, recruitment and retention of world-class students and scholars, professional development and employability, innovation, and social responsibility?

No matter where they may be in this journey, readers will do well to attend to the lessons shared by the authors and contributors in the pages that follow.

Jeffrey M. Riedinger, PhD, is the vice provost for global affairs and professor of law at the University of Washington in Seattle. He serves as the 2021–22 NAFSA president and chair of the Board of Directors.

References

ICEF Monitor. 2017. "OECD Charts a Slowing of International Mobility Growth." September 20. https://monitor.icef.com/2017/09/oecd-charts-slowing-international-mobility-growth/.

Organisation for Economic Co-operation and Development (OECD). 2020. "Indicator B6. What Is the Profile of Internationally Mobile Students?" *Education at a Glance 2020: OECD Indicators.* https://www.oecd-ilibrary.org/sites/69096873-en/1/3/3/6/index.html?itemId=/content/publication/69096873-en&_csp_=b68ed930151b9d0f354aa48ee27178db&itemIGO=oecd&itemContentType=book.

Introduction

Meaningful experiences lead individuals to form strong connections with people and places, return to them, and continually support them. This holds true for international students and alumni and their educational experiences. Personal experience is a main point of reference and, when that experience is meaningful—one that is thoughtful, satisfying, respectful, and beneficial—students and alumni may decide to invest in a lifetime relationship with their alma mater. International alumni engagement is defined in many ways across different constituencies and cultures, and some experiences as students— and international alumni—will matter more than others.

As we started writing this book in summer 2020, members of the Riga Technical University (RTU) Alumni Association, which is located in Latvia, co-organized with their alma mater the Grand Drive-In Graduation for the thousand graduates to receive their diplomas. Their families and friends could watch the ceremony live on the RTU web page, its Facebook page, and the national public TV channel. It was moving to see how these new alumni expressed their joy, dancing next to their cars and waving at each other triumphantly; despite the pandemic, they were able to complete their degrees. RTU and its alumni association's efforts and creativity in finding a meaningful way to welcome recent graduates into their alumni community will surely resonate not only with these new alumni but also with their families, friends, and local and global communities. This is an experience that will matter to these recent graduates—now alumni.

As international educators, we know that studying and living abroad demand a broad mindset, flexibility, introspection, willingness to deal with uncertainty, and especially a disposition open to new friendships. Across decades of working with international students and alumni, we have experienced the many ways international alumni cherish their alma mater, want to help build international bridges, and contribute to their communities back home and abroad.

Sandra's Story

When I worked as director of international relations for the Tilburg School of Economics and Management, the department trained many international students as volunteers and part-time employees to help with our campus activities. Years later, as director of international alumni relations, all those former international students who volunteered and worked with us helped our team build the university's international alumni program. With their support, we were able to establish international alumni chapters in China, Colombia, and Turkey in the early years of the program. These alumni chapters enabled Tilburg University, located in the Netherlands, to expand its collaboration with partner universities in student exchange, dual degrees in undergraduate and graduate programs, and research projects. Our international alumni co-organized events with us, connected us with key players in the private sector and governmental agencies, represented the university at student fairs, recruited students, and kept us informed of new developments whenever they saw opportunities for us to collaborate. I'm frequently inspired by the generous spirit of the many international alumni I have met and continue to get to know in my daily work.

Gretchen's Story

International alumni from Tufts University in the United States were similarly involved in helping expand the university's reputation and relationships abroad. I spent some of my most rewarding career years developing a comprehensive international engagement strategy which, a decade later, continues to attract support and resources from Tufts's leadership, graduate, and undergraduate programs; faculty; and international alumni, families, and strategic partners such as government offices abroad. There is nothing more fulfilling than knowing the investments made in international alumni chapter leadership development for the past 20 years have been recognized when, for example, one of the original London Tufts Alliance leaders became the president of the Tufts University Alumni Association.

Our Call to Action

Together, we want to challenge readers to think about what success means when it comes to internationalization and international alumni relations: What is the overall purpose of engaging alumni (and future alumni)? What is the institution trying to achieve? How does it measure progress? Through many years of building international alumni strategies, we know that international alumni are undertapped (or untapped) resources, and once institutions invest in and nurture their international alumni communities, these networks can support internationalization and much more.

The Growing Importance of International Alumni

Before the Fourth Industrial Revolution and the advent of social media more than 20 years ago, a very small percentage of educational institutions attracted and retained their international alumni, families, and key stakeholders through in-person relationship-building. Those that did were primarily independent secondary schools with sizable percentages of international students and ongoing recruitment activity as well as elite higher educational institutions benefiting from mature fundraising efforts. Now, prospective international students—and domestic students seeking study abroad opportunities—increasingly consult information and evaluate other students' experiences via social media. While this increase in access to online information and virtual events creates new opportunities for institutions to engage international students and alumni, it also means international educators, recruitment teams, and alumni engagement professionals have more responsibilities than ever before.

Much has changed since the turn of the twenty-first century, as institutions around the world began developing advancement functions focusing on external relationships with alumni and donors. Some of the activity has revolved around organizing in-person speaker events with leaders and prominent faculty; inviting alumni to help build and join in-person and online communities; and extending opportunities to support international student recruitment, host international student internships, and donate to international student scholarships. Other institutional initiatives leverage relationships with highly engaged international alumni to raise awareness, support, and funds for humanitarian causes or disaster relief.

Then, in 2020, the world experienced the COVID-19 pandemic, and the international higher education sector recognized very different realities with respect to international alumni relations, emblematic of the diversity that exists across institutions, countries, and regions. Institutions with engaged and supportive international alumni could draw on relationships built over years of engagement and deploy volunteers to aid them during the crisis with crowdfunding, collecting masks and other personal protective equipment for hospitals, and supporting international students financially and emotionally, just to mention a few. Others with more nascent programs may have prioritized different advancement activities over international alumni engagement and, as a result, did not have the resources for an international alumni outreach plan.

On the whole, however, the pandemic has sparked a growing interest across the world in developing relationships with international alumni and widening the circle of participation between constituents. Many more players have begun to focus on the influence of international alumni and the positive difference they can make during times of uncertainty or calm. Institutions are developing domestic and international advancement programs, cross-functional volunteer programs (international alumni student recruitment, career development, civic engagement), and national or regional partnerships to serve both short- and long-term internationalization goals. This book reaffirms the value proposition for international alumni engagement and how a variety of stakeholders with a shared sense of purpose serves as a catalyst for positive societal impact, both locally and globally.

A Fresh Look at International Alumni Relations

Engaging International Alumni as Strategic Partners is NAFSA's first book on the subject of international alumni engagement to advance comprehensive internationalization. We have leveraged our expertise and academic knowledge in international higher education to compose a book that builds a case for why institutions should invest in international alumni engagement, how they can establish an alumni program, and what can be learned from other professionals engaging international alumni. Throughout the book, a diverse set of guest contributors from around the world present institutional and organizational models and case studies for building affinity and support among international alumni who, in turn, demonstrate their sense of belonging, knowledge, and ability to influence and create change. The following presents a brief description of each of the six chapters.

Chapter 1, "Why Higher Education Should Engage International Alumni," provides an overview of how international alumni in their many roles can help their alma mater contribute to a global society in meaningful ways. International alumni can advance the institution's strategy to serve society, attract and retain global talent, and bring tremendous economic and humanistic values to their host and home countries. These are just some of the strategic and altruistic reasons for positioning international alumni relations as a key driver in advancing internationalization.

Chapter 2, "International Alumni Relations Program Development," provides a framework for cultivating an international alumni relations program and explores the types of investments required to sustain these programs. The discussion begins by defining different types of roles international alumni assume, from advisers to ambassadors. Next, the chapter introduces the role of international alumni chapters and considerations for those interested in developing—and sustaining—overseas communities. An additional theme is the notion that international alumni relations program development requires strong alignment between internal stakeholders and external stakeholders in a strategic country. Mapping both types of stakeholders provides a context for activating international alumni relations programs.

Chapter 3, "A Framework for Growing and Maintaining International Alumni Engagement," highlights the importance of cultivating relationships with international students and international alumni. The international student experience is a critical time for institutions to extend their support networks, as future graduates' perceptions and experiences can influence their desires to remain active alumni. The rest of the chapter utilizes the LEARN Model to guide international education decision-makers along the international alumni life cycle.

Chapter 4, "International Alumni Ambassador Programs," discusses what is meant by international alumni ambassador affinity and support. Additionally, it reviews how international alumni ambassadors communicate, build relationships and networks, and engage with stakeholders in the age of social media. A discussion of the types of training and other investments required to attract and retain international alumni ambassadors who carry forward the institution's brands and messaging rounds out the chapter.

Chapter 5, "Transformational Philanthropy: Alumni Giving to Advance the International Agenda," focuses on the intersection between philanthropy, alumni engagement, and internationalization, and presents examples of how alumni contributions (both monetary and nonmonetary) enhance internationalization and support international outreach efforts. It presents a three-pronged framework for institutions to make strong cases for international alumni involvement in philanthropic efforts. Recent stories speak to the COVID-19 era, when international alumni supported international students in vulnerable positions with bursaries and much-needed emergency funds. Other examples discuss why international alumni who share a common experience—whether they be from the same home country, exchange, or academic program—value supporting internationalization efforts or other campus initiatives.

Chapter 6, "Roles of International Alumni: Perspectives from the Field," is composed of four sections that provide model practice examples from around the world of the impact of cultivating international alumni relationships. International education professionals offer their advice and share their stories on (1) brand and reputation management, (2) recruitment and retention of talent, (3) professional development and employability in the twenty-first century, and (4) innovation and social responsibility.

Audience for the Publication

Engaging International Alumni as Strategic Partners is written for decision-makers who have an interest in leveraging the potential for more engaged international alumni and a desire to apply model practices to their institution, nonprofit, or other governmental or industry settings. Such readers may include
- **deans and managers of international programs** striving to develop an institution-wide approach to international alumni and constituent relations;
- **directors of international enrollment management, international student services, and admissions offices** seeking alternative ways to recruit international students and engage families, agents, and other stakeholders;
- **directors of alumni relations programs** interested in starting an international alumni strategy or department;
- **new international alumni relations professionals** (central, faculty, or school-based) eager to expand their knowledge of the field;
- **experienced international alumni relations professionals** seeking expert knowledge and capacity;
- **international education professionals** interested in understanding the value proposition of international alumni relations;
- **communications and marketing professionals** responsible for disseminating the "global story" of institutions as well as managing branding campaigns; and

- **associations, consortia, governments, and other organizations** with strong alumni beneficiary and support networks.

We hope the themes and model practice examples in the book inspire additional research and professional development activities in international alumni relations. The overall call to action is for all readers to contribute in engaging international alumni more consistently and effectively as strategic partners in internationalization.

A Final Thought on Belonging and Contributing

International alumni engagement is ultimately about one's feelings of belonging and contributing. Award-winning author Howard Ross (2018) describes the notion of belonging as a sense of shared identity, a shared destiny, a sense of interdependence, a sense of shared values, and an ability for individuals to express their authentic self. An alma mater is a place where an academic community consisting of students, faculty, staff, and alumni shares a common identity, values, interdependence, and destiny. Engaging international alumni and instilling an enduring sense of belonging build the trust and space for individuals to continue to express their authentic self regardless of geography.

In the current and future international higher education landscape, international student participation will continue to increase in numbers; geographical representation; and cultural, racial, and gender diversity. More students participating in international exchange and obtaining degrees in person or online from institutions outside their home country results in more international alumni. Some will remain in their host country for graduate programs, obtain jobs, and seek residency. As international educators, we care for our international students, and we should want our international alumni to feel that they belong and matter. With higher education's responsibility for helping to solve global challenges, the opportunities to create and nurture meaningful relationships with our international alumni have never been more important.

Reference

Ross, Howard J. 2018. *Our Search for Belonging*. Oakland, CA: Berrett-Koehler Publishers.

Chapter 1

Why Higher Education Should Engage International Alumni

In an era of globalization, many universities face common challenges: fierce competition for the best students and academics; branding and institutional reputation abroad; pressure to move up (and stay up) in world rankings; rising tuition fees; escalating student debt; and tight governmental and institutional budgets. With the increased liberalization of public higher education, the decline of state funding, and the worldwide demonstrations for social justice, many questions come to mind for the majority of universities with international ambitions: How can higher education institutions maintain a high quality of education and research while demonstrating societal impact, not only locally but also globally? How can they best attract and retain national and international students to provide diverse, multicultural, and inclusive programs? How can they offer a transformative experience to empower their students for meaningful careers as global citizens?

University leadership, faculty, staff, and international educators continually seek answers to these questions regarding the mission of higher education institutions and internationalization, in other words their *raison d'être*. A university's mission defines its identity, position locally and globally, core activities, and priorities. Now, most universities integrate internationalization into their purpose, functions, or delivery of education, not only to enhance the quality of their education and research but also to meaningfully contribute to society (Knight 2008; de Wit et al. 2015).

International alumni—as former international students, former exchange students, or expats abroad—can play a strategic role in helping universities advance their internationalization strategy. Given that international alumni work in private and public sectors around the world, they can open, bridge, and build many relationships within their communities in partnership with their alma mater.

Chapter 1

This chapter provides an overview of how international alumni, in their many roles, can serve higher education's service mission and help institutions contribute in meaningful ways to local and global societies. The following sections build a case for support to aid international educators and alumni relations professionals in creating or expanding international alumni engagement and to hone the goals of existing international alumni programs.

Higher Education's Service Mission

Before widespread globalization and the development of the knowledge economy, the roles of higher education institutions were primarily teaching and research (Frondizi et al. 2019). Now, as active agents in producing and circulating new knowledge and talent within the information economy, universities are challenged to take a more active and responsible role in serving society. Many scholars refer to serving society as the university's third mission, which involves transferring academic knowledge to the wider community in the form of workshops and professional development courses, as well as establishing partnerships between educational institutions and the private and public sectors (Laredo 2007; Montesinos et al. 2008).

Together with international alumni, universities can cocreate new programs, such as workshops and guest lectures on topics that connect academic knowledge with challenges faced by other countries. In addition, international alumni can serve the third mission in many roles, such as advisers to help develop curricula that bring in multicultural perspectives, liaisons to build partnerships for their alma mater's academic programs and research back in their home countries, and mentors and employers to open opportunities to current students in a global market. In other words, international alumni can assist universities in serving local and global societies.

Research on how international alumni incorporate their overseas education when giving back to their home country suggests that international alumni networks are fundamental. A study by Campbell and Baxter (2019) shows that international scholarship recipients commonly enact social change back in their home country through alumni associations. The authors define social change as "societal shifts that are focused on the social, emotional, and personal development of the individuals within the society, believed to be moving towards 'progress.'

Social change includes increased attention and support for all—especially those at the margins—and often addresses issues of education, human rights, and health services" (Campbell and Baxter 2019, 1).

An example of such an initiative is the International Fellows Program Alumni Association of Ghana (IFPAAG), which was launched in 2007 with the theme of "Championing Social Justice" with support from the Ford Foundation and the Association of African Universities. IFPAAG focuses on promoting social justice in Ghana by providing a forum where alumni can support each other's social change projects, raise awareness on specific social issues, and build skills and knowledge among members.

International alumni networks often support social change and address systemic inequalities by fundraising for scholarships for marginalized students (Garchitorena 2007), leading community service events (Farrow and Yuan 2011), providing humanitarian aid (Hanson 2005), and influencing national policy (Campbell and Baxter 2019). Higher education's service mission entails engaging with global society, and international alumni associations can help advance social change when their members return to their home countries.

Talent and Innovation

In addition to promoting higher education's service mission at home and abroad, many institutions and national governments are concerned with how higher education can generate innovation to stay globally competitive. The Organisation for Economic Co-operation and Development's (OECD) Indicators of Talent Attractiveness is an online tool that allows OECD countries to measure their capacity to attract and retain three types of talented migrants: highly educated workers (those with master's and doctoral degrees), foreign entrepreneurs, and university students. Since 2015, the annual *Global Talent Competitiveness Index (GTCI)* has compared more than 120 countries on different aspects of growing and retaining talent (Lanvin and Evans 2018) and their ability to stay at the forefront of innovation.

International students, and therefore international alumni, are integral to a country's success in these areas. For example, the OECD's 2016 report pointed to the Netherlands's need to attract and retain international talent to stay competitive in the knowledge economy. Furthermore, the 2018 *GTCI* report ranked the

Netherlands as the world's top country in growing talent, but ranked it ninth in the overall ranking because it lags behind in attracting and retaining international talent (Lanvin and Evans 2018). From 2013 to 2016, Nuffic (the Dutch organization for internationalization in education) coordinated a program called Make it in the Netherlands to engage international talent before, during, and after their studies in the Netherlands, believing that retention of international alumni benefits the country's knowledge economy. The program was divided into five action lines: (1) Dutch language learning; (2) connection between study and the labor market; (3) a buddy system to connect internationals with Dutch citizens; (4) a transparent administrative process to apply for internships and jobs; and (5) support of regional programs that include internationals.

Of great importance, Nuffic's Make it in the Netherlands supported the launch of an international student and alumni association in the Netherlands. In 2018, Nuffic presented a national strategy to engage international alumni at home and abroad as key actors (Nuffic 2018a). These initiatives have contributed to Nuffic's and Dutch higher education institutions' ongoing efforts in attracting and retaining international talent. Nuffic's latest report on international student mobility shows that 12.5 percent of all enrolled degree-seeking students were international in the 2019–20 academic year. This is an increase of 2 percent since 2018–19 (Nuffic 2020). The number of alumni joining the NL alumni network has also kept growing, with a total of 80 associations representing different countries. These local associations help brand and spread the reputation of Dutch higher education globally. The NL alumni network-Netherlands, the association for international students and alumni residing in the Netherlands, has also seen a growing number of members, with a total of 4,000 at the start of 2021.

Talented, skilled, and innovative international alumni play a key role in a country's prosperity—not only contributing to stronger economic growth but also to maintaining the country's attractiveness to international talent. Of the 29,500 prospective international students surveyed in the 2020 QS *International Student Survey*, 40 percent stated they consulted alumni from universities they were interested in when deciding where to study. As the research states, "We should consider the importance of international alumni networks here, as the potential to attract new international students through word-of-mouth recommendations is significant" (QS 2020, 45).

Economic Impact

The number of students studying outside their home country increased from 2 million in 1998 to 5.3 million by 2017 (OECD 2019, 231). Research undertaken for IDP Education in Australia in 2007, and still widely cited (Preece 2018), suggests that roughly 7.2 million students will be pursuing some higher education internationally by 2025 at a compound annual growth rate of 5.8 percent (Banks, Olsen, and Pearce 2007, 14). Less optimistically, a British Council (2018) report projects the annual growth for global outbound students will actually drop from the 5.7 percent seen from 2000 to 2015 to an average of 1.7 percent by 2027. These figures do not include the impact of the COVID-19 pandemic on the global student mobility trends. Still, the increase in international student mobility, whether large or small, also means an increase in the number of international alumni that universities can connect with and engage.

Rahul Choudaha (2019) estimates that the 5.1 million international students studying in tertiary education have a global economic impact of $300 billion. NAFSA's 2020 economic analysis in the United States shows that for every eight international students, three jobs were created or supported by the money students spent in higher education, accommodations, dining, retail, transportation, telecommunications, and health insurance, contributing $38.7 billion to the U.S. economy.

Although not all international students stay to live and work in their host country after graduation, reports show that those who do continue to have a large economic impact, even just through what they pay in taxes. In 2019, a report commissioned by Kaplan International Pathways and the Higher Education Policy Institute estimated the United Kingdom's tax revenues collected £3.2 billion from just one cohort of international alumni who stayed to work in the country (Conlon, Halterbeck, and Hedges 2019). A Nuffic report estimated the retention of 19 percent of international alumni generated €1.64 billion for the Dutch treasury every year (Nuffic 2018b, 16).

International alumni can also financially contribute to their alma mater through philanthropy. In response to COVID-19, many higher education institutions saw abundant examples of how domestic and international alumni helped their local communities by volunteering time and knowledge or donating money to emergency funds. For example, a professor from the University of Texas-Dallas (UT Dallas), who was an international student himself, reached out to alumni to gain support for the university's COVID-19 relief fund. UT Dallas alumni donated almost $50,000 to help international students during the crisis. As one UT alum who donated to the relief fund said, "Right now, these international students are going through a storm. When they come out of it, they will excel. They will be useful for our community, for the United States, and for the tech field. I wanted to be a part of that push through to help them keep their momentum" (Steele 2020).

By attracting international talent to higher education, universities are not only large contributors to the national gross domestic product, but when international graduates stay to work and live in their host country, universities also have long-term socioeconomic impact by bringing financial wealth and human capital to their nation. International alumni have also proved great proponents of philanthropy initiatives and give back in a multitude of ways.

Global Problem-Solving

Beyond the economic benefits of attracting and retaining international talent, one of internationalization's fundamental and much-needed contributions is educating citizens to be globally engaged and socially responsible—and international alumni can be a leading force. Even though over the past 30 years the internationalization of higher education in many countries has developed to a more comprehensive component of higher education policy and practices (de Wit and Rumbley 2017), it is still vulnerable to socioeconomic and political forces. As so many international educators can attest, geopolitical climates of anti-immigration, racial, religious, and political turmoil create anti-internationalization discourses in favor of nationalism. Despite some nations looking inward, the 2030 Agenda for Sustainable Development of the United Nations established 17 Sustainable Development Goals (SDGs) that aim to end poverty, protect the planet, and promote prosperity through global collaboration (UN 2015). The European Association of Universities emphasizes higher education's pivotal role in partnering with civil society to provide added value in meeting the SDGs (Jorgensen 2019).

Some universities are embracing their commitment to include SDGs in education by engaging students, academic units, and staff—and international alumni (Kestin et al. 2017). The second edition of the Times Higher Education (THE) Impact Ranking in 2020 assessed 766 universities across 85 countries against the 17 SDGs. Leading the Impact Rankings for the second time in a row, New Zealand's University of Auckland outlines its contribution to achieving SDGs in its

Sustainability Report 2019 (UA 2019). As part of its commitment to sustainability, the University of Auckland's Alumni Relations Office launched its first Volunteer Impact Week (VIW) in 2019. Attracting hundreds of alumni around the globe to volunteer, this initiative provided them with opportunities to have an impact on sustainability in communities across New Zealand and the world. One of the results was a book drive for Tongan children, Books4Tonga. As Joel Terwilliger, alumni relations manager and founder of VIW, explains, "It's amazing how when people collectively take action on issues they care about, the impact we can have. Books4Tonga is a good example of how we can change a corner of the world pretty easily. It gives us real impetus to try more events next year." For the 2020 VIW, the Alumni Relations Office teamed up with Volunteering New Zealand (an association of volunteer centers and national and regional organizations) to support their shared commitment to sustainability. The alumni relations website for volunteering and mentoring lists many projects where alumni can donate their time to flora and fauna, health and the elderly, education and international students, gender equality, and more.

International alumni are also joining their former host countries in initiatives that support the SDGs. For example, the DAAD (German Academic Exchange Service) manages Germany's global alumni network, Alumniportal Deutschland, of more than 150,000 international alumni and stakeholders in 2020. Alumniportal Deutschland's international alumni are referred to as Germany Alumni and include anyone from any nationality who studied, worked, did research, or completed a training program or a German-language course at a German institution. The Alumniportal Deutschland's Global Goals initiative highlights Germany Alumni stories across all 17 SDGs in an eBook titled *The Global Goals—Powered by Alumni*. These stories, written in German, showcase international alumni who have returned to their home country and are making an impact as environmentalists, activists, social entrepreneurs, and more (Alumniportal Deutschland 2018). For example, Gladys Mosomtai, an environmental scientist and a DAAD scholarship recipient from Kenya, researches the population dynamics of pests infesting coffee plants:

> I analyze the conditions favorable to pests and diseases, and investigate the influence of environmental factors. The objective is to provide the region's farmers with recommendations and help them to avoid pest-related

losses by employing cultivation methods adapted to the environmental conditions. I wish to use my academic expertise to help solve African problems. (Mittelstraß 2019)

Rosaleda Reynoso, who is from the Dominican Republic, has a PhD in engineering science from the University of Stuttgart and is a professor, architect, and social entrepreneur. She founded Casita para la Vida (Little House of Life) to build adequate living spaces for families in rural and urban areas of the Dominican Republic. In July 2015, Casita para la Vida was awarded first place in the Alumniportal Deutschland's Mission Responsible competition, which invited Germany Alumni to showcase their commitment to social and ecological issues (Köster 2015). These Germany Alumni not only help Germany, their home countries, and local communities advance SDGs but also assist their alma mater in showing the impact higher education institutions can have around the world through their international alumni.

The SDGs are unique in that they call for action by all countries. International alumni are obvious strategic partners to higher education institutions in contributing to the SDGs because they can help build and maintain global relations. They can contribute the academic knowledge, intercultural competence, social responsibility, and entrepreneurial mindset needed to promote peace, international collaboration, and solutions to global issues. Engaging international alumni locally and abroad to cocreate solutions and social movements through knowledge exchange and better cultural understanding fosters the humanistic aspects of internationalization. Given their unique connections to local and global communities and networks, international alumni can advance issues that cannot be solved by one university or nation alone.

Conclusion

As shown throughout this chapter, universities need their international alumni networks to fulfill their service mission, attract global talent and innovation, gain economic benefits, and work to solve global problems. Some nations have also realized that international alumni can be effective liaisons to support internationalization of higher education, their country brand, SDGs, public diplomacy, and civic engagement (Rincón and Rutkowski 2015). Universities can benefit from aligning efforts with the public and private sectors to expand their international alumni networks. Engaging them strategically can open economic opportunities; spark and generate innovation; promote academic, professional, and cultural knowledge exchange; and brand higher education abroad. All these benefits can aid in making a case for creating, reshaping, and sustaining international alumni programs. Students have a temporary stay on campus but continue to be alumni forever.

References

Alumniportal Deutschland. 2018. *The Global Goal—Powered by Alumni*. https://www.alumniportal-deutschland.org/fileadmin/bilder/nachhaltigkeit/sdg/allgemein/sdg-e-book-powered-by-alumni.pdf.

Banks, Melissa, Alan Olsen, and David Pearce. 2007. *Global Student Mobility: An Australian Perspective Five Years On*. IDP Education. http://www.spre.com.au/download/IDPResearch2007.pdf.

British Council. 2018. "International Student Mobility to Grow More Slowly to 2027." February 1. https://www.britishcouncil.org/contact/press/international-student-mobility-grow-more-slowly-2027.

Campbell, Anne C., and Aryn R. Baxter. 2019. "Exploring the Attributes and Practices of Alumni Associations that Advance Social Change." *International Journal of Educational Development* 66:164–72.

Choudaha, Rahul. 2019. "Beyond $300 Billion: The Global Impact of International Students." *Studyportals*. https://studyportals.com/intelligence/global-impact-of-international-students/.

Conlon, Gavan, Maike Halterbeck, and Sophie Hedges. 2019. *The UK's Tax Revenues from International Students Post-graduation*. The Higher Education Policy Institute and Kaplan International Pathways. https://www.hepi.ac.uk/wp-content/uploads/2019/03/The-UK-tax-revenues-from-international-students.pdf.

de Wit, Hans, Fiona Hunter, Laura Howard, and Eva Egron-Polak. 2015. *Internationalisation of Higher Education*. Brussels: European Parliament. https://www.europarl.europa.eu/RegData/etudes/STUD/2015/540370/IPOL_STU(2015)540370_EN.pdf.

de Wit, Hans, and Laura Rumbley. 2017. "Professional Development in International Education: The Example of Boston College MA in International Higher Education." *Internationalisation of Higher Education* 3:2–14.

Farrow, Harmonie, and Y. Corrine Yuan. 2011. "Building Stronger Ties with Alumni Through Facebook to Increase Volunteerism and Charitable Giving." *Journal of Computer-Mediated Communication* 16, 3:445–64.

Frondizi, Rocco, Chiara Fantauzzi, Nathalie Colasanti, and Gloria Fiorani. 2019. "The Evaluation of Universities' Third Mission and Intellectual Capital: Theoretical Analysis and Application to Italy." *Sustainability* 11, 12:3455.

Garchitorena, Victoria P. 2007. *Diaspora Philanthropy: The Philippine Experience*. The Philanthropic Initiative, Inc. and The Global Equity Initiative, Harvard University. http://www.tpi.org/sites/default/files/pdf/philippines.

Hanson, Kobena T. 2005. "Landscapes of Survival and Escape: Social Networking and Urban Livelihoods in Ghana." *Environment and Planning A* 37, 7:1291–310.

Jorgensen, Thomas. 2019. "Universities Move to Achieve the SDGs—and Approach the Next Hurdle." European University Association. May 16. https://eua.eu/resources/expert-voices/110:universities-move-to-achieve-the-sdgs-%E2%80%93-and-approach-the-next-hurdle.html.

Kestin, Tahl, Marjan van den Belt, Leanne Denby, Katie Ross, John Thwaites, and Martine Hawkes. 2017. *Getting Started with the SDGs in Universities*. Sustainable Development Solutions Network—Australia/Pacific, Australasian Campuses Towards Sustainability, and the Global SDSN Secretariat. August 22. https://resources.unsdsn.org/getting-started-with-the-sdgs-in-universities.

Knight, Jane. 2008. *Higher Education in Turmoil: The Changing World of Internationalization*. Rotterdam, The Netherlands: Sense Publishers.

Köster, Thomas. 2015. "#MissionResponsible: Rosaleda Reynoso on 'Casita para la Vida.'" Alumniportal Deutschland. https://www.alumniportal-deutschland.org/en/alumni-stories/interviews/germany-alumni-rosaleda-reynoso-casita-para-la-vida/.

Lanvin, Bruno, and Paul Evans, eds. 2018. *The Global Talent Competitive Index 2018*. INSEAD, the Adecco Group, and Tata Communications. https://www.insead.edu/sites/default/files/assets/dept/globalindices/docs/GTCI-2018-report.pdf.

Laredo, Philippe. 2007. "Revisiting the Third Mission of Universities: Toward a Renewed Categorization of University Activities?" *Higher Education Policy* 20, 1:441–56.

Mittelstraß, Bettina. 2019. "'Kenya Needs Me.'" Alumniportal Deutschland. https://www.alumniportal-deutschland.org/en/alumni-stories/interviews/kenya-needs-me/.

Montesinos, Patricio, Jose Miguel Carot, Juan Miguel Martínez, and F. J. Mora. 2008. "Third Mission Ranking for World Class Universities: Beyond Teaching and Research." *Higher Education in Europe* 33, 2:259–71.

NAFSA: Association of International Educators. 2019. "New NAFSA Data: Despite Stagnant Enrollment, International Students Contribute Nearly $41 Billion to the U.S. Economy." November 18. https://www.nafsa.org/about/about-nafsa/new-nafsa-data-despite-stagnant-enrollment.

NAFSA: Association of International Educators. 2020. "The United States of America Benefits from International Students." https://www.nafsa.org/sites/default/files/media/document/isev-2020.pdf.

Nuffic. 2018a. *A National Alumni Strategy*. July 13. https://www.nuffic.nl/en/publications/national-alumni-strategy.

Nuffic. 2018b. "Stayrate van Internationale Afgestudeerden in Nederland." October 5. https://www.nuffic.nl/publicaties/stayrate-van-internationale-afgestudeerden-nederland.

Nuffic. 2020. *How Is COVID-19 Affecting International Students' Plans to Study in the Netherlands?* The Hague, The Netherlands: Nuffic. https://www.nuffic.nl/sites/default/files/2020-08/how-is-covid-19-affecting-international-students-plans-to-study-in-the-netherlands.pdf.

Organisation for Economic Co-operation and Development (OECD). 2016. *Recruiting Immigrant Workers: The Netherlands 2016*. Paris, France: OECD Publishing. https://www.oecd.org/migration/recruiting-immigrant-workers-the-netherlands-2016-9789264259249-en.htm.

Organisation for Economic Co-operation and Development (OECD). 2019. *Education at a Glance 2019: OECD Indicators*. Paris: OECD Publishing. https://www.oecd-ilibrary.org/education/education-at-a-glance-2019_f8d7880d-en.

Preece, Alan. 2018. "8 Million Globally Mobile Students—A Myth, Based on a Rounding Error, Sustained by Wishful Thinking?" *View from a Bridge*, February 13. https://www.viewfromabridge.org/2018/02/13/8-million-globally-mobile-students-a-myth-based-on-a-rounding-error-sustained-by-wishful-thinking/.

QS. 2020. *International Student Survey: Global Opportunities in the New Higher Education Paradigm*. QS and the European Union. https://info.qs.com/rs/335-VIN-535/images/QS_EU_Universities_Edition-International_Student_Survey_2020.pdf.

Rincón, Sandra, and Anne Rutkowski. 2015. "The National Agenda and International Alumni Relations: Strategies of Engagement for the Future of European Higher Education." In *Staying Global: How International Alumni Relations Advances the Agenda*, ed. Gretchen Dobson. EAIE Occasional Paper 24.

Steele, Daniel. 2020. "Alumni Rally Around International Students." University of Texas-Dallas Office of Development and Alumni Relations. June 8. https://www.utdallas.edu/development/alumni-rally-around-international-students/.

Times Higher Education. 2020. "The Times Higher Education Impact Rankings." https://www.timeshighereducation.com/rankings/impact/2020/overall#!/page/0/length/25/sort_by/rank/sort_order/asc/cols/undefined.

United Nations. 2015. *Transforming Our World: The 2030 Agenda for Sustainable Development*. https://sustainabledevelopment.un.org/content/documents/21252030%20Agenda%20for%20Sustainable%20Development%20web.pdf.

University of Auckland (UA). 2019. *The University of Auckland: Sustainability Report 2019*. https://cdn.auckland.ac.nz/assets/auckland/about-us/the-university/sustainability-and-environment/sustainability-development-goals/SDG%20Booklet%20Web.pdf.

Chapter 2
International Alumni Relations Program Development

Before developing an international alumni relations program, universities should consider why such a program is necessary and how it will support its mission and international strategy. The previous chapter offered various arguments for why universities should engage their international alumni. To further build a case for support and bring a university's leadership, faculty, and other administrative staff on board, elaborating a strategy is necessary. This chapter describes the fundamental elements essential in building a strategy. A first step is to determine who will be included when defining international alumni and what roles they can play in supporting the university's international agenda. A following step is to consider establishing international alumni chapters, their locations, and their roles in branding and representing their institution abroad. This section on international alumni chapters elaborates on four core components of a chapter's governance: mission and objectives, leadership, volunteer management, and budget. The next section discusses mapping and gaining internal and external stakeholders' support for a successful program. Finally, the last section reviews the importance of defining key performance indicators to evaluate the return on investment. The chapter concludes with a case study of KU Leuven that captures how an international alumni strategy can be interwoven with comprehensive internationalization to support the university's vision for a sustainable society.

Defining International Alumni

Universities define international alumni differently. Many include former and current incoming and outgoing exchange students, international students who completed a full degree (bachelor's, master's, or doctoral), those who completed certificate programs from professional schools, and expatriate graduates living abroad. Universities should decide on a definition that will serve the objectives of the international alumni relations program, internationalization goals, and the institution overall.

For example, if a university is just starting to internationalize and does not have international graduates of degree programs, then current and former exchange students may be included in the university's definition of international alumni. Former exchange students can be engaged to help advance internationalization goals, such as branding the university and its programs abroad, attracting more international students, and expanding exchange programs. Thanks to two former exchange students from Germany who helped develop a web page to promote its exchange program and benefits, Durban University of Technology (DUT) in South Africa has increased its number of German exchange students from two to more than 100 in recent years. According to Lavern Samuels (2020), director of international education and partnership, these two former exchange students return every 2 years to DUT to review their work and learn how else they can keep supporting the university.

Institutions that segment their alumni demographics as domestic or international may consider a third category to define and engage international alumni who conduct their personal and professional lives within two or more countries: transnational alumni (Dobson 2015). Transnational communities provide valuable resources for institutions committed to comprehensive internationalization. Throughout this book, transnational alumni are included under the umbrella term of "international alumni."

International Alumni Roles

International alumni can play many roles as they share networks, knowledge, and expertise and advance the university's international strategy. Figure 1 categorizes different alumni roles and the topics they encompass.

Figure 1. Alumni Roles

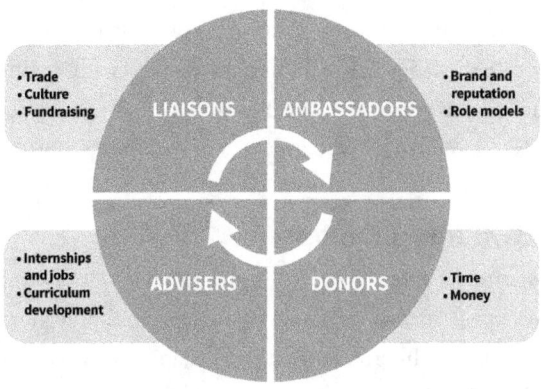

Liaisons

International alumni can open doors to their employers or companies to facilitate internships, jobs, and donations for student scholarships. They can also foment cross-cultural understanding and goodwill to create bridges with other universities and the public and private sectors.

Ambassadors

International alumni can help promote the institution's brand, reputation, educational programs, and research in their home country. They can share their knowledge and expertise in their fields as role models to future students and young alumni through lectures and testimonials. (For more on international alumni ambassadors, see chapter 4.)

Donors

International alumni can donate their time by volunteering for many types of activities, from organizing networking sessions to building an alumni chapter. They can also invest their expertise and money in supporting their alma mater's initiatives in their home country and help fundraise for scholarships for other international students. (For more on international alumni as donors, see chapter 5.)

Advisers
International alumni can be advisers or mentors to students and recent graduates on how to navigate the labor market. They can also offer advice on competencies and skills needed in their country or field of work as well as new developments in their professional sector.

International Alumni Chapters
International alumni chapters refer to formal networks of alumni representing their alma mater in a particular city, country, or geographical region, or worldwide through virtual chapters. International alumni chapters can also be referred to as international alumni clubs, communities, or networks, and in addition to their geographical basis, they can be organized by academic discipline or professional themes. International alumni networks have a formal organizational structure with notarized bylaws and, at times, include chapters of their own in different cities throughout their country or region.

Establishing an international alumni chapter abroad or online requires mutual collaboration between the university and international alumni leaders. A relationship based on a horizontal share of power benefits both the university and international alumni leaders. The 2019 *Chapter Benchmarking* report by billhighway and Mariner Management & Marketing, which tracks chapter trends since 2016, shows that alumni chapters have become essential for member engagement. In addition, the report states that virtual learning and professional development help boost engagement at the local level. The report's researchers further explain that alumni chapters are critical channels for both educational and networking opportunities, which can be delivered through a hybrid approach: in-person and online learning events using local components (e.g., a webinar between face-to-face meetings). International alumni chapters can help build a two-way relationship, bringing faraway alumni closer to their alma mater.

The Role of International Alumni Chapters
Most universities establish alumni chapters abroad to engage their international alumni in expanding their brand and building their reputation, recruiting international students, finding out-of-touch alumni, sourcing internships, and growing a network of mentors in a particular country—as well as offering an

international community to their students and alumni. A chapter can create an environment to share knowledge, career advancement, and business partnerships for alumni and future alumni (current students). It can also foster a climate of pride and support for current and future students, the university, and the international alumni. It is always important to survey alumni in a particular country to adapt programming to their local needs.

Figure 2 shows the three main goals that commonly inform international alumni chapters' programming: (1) building their alma mater's brand and reputation; (2) offering professional development and networking opportunities; and (3) locally promoting social impact and fundraising.

Figure 2. International Alumni Chapter's Strategic Pillars

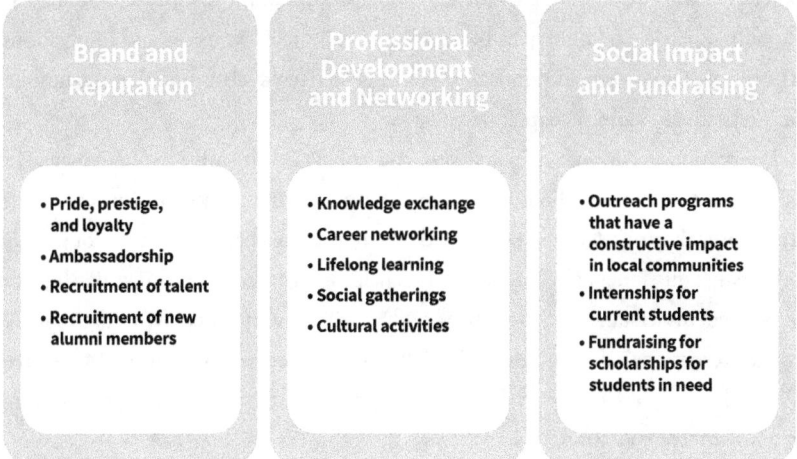

Chapter Governance

There are four core components the university and alumni leaders must consider when establishing an international alumni relations program and alumni chapters: mission and objectives, leadership, volunteer management, and budget.

Mission and Objectives

As a first step in developing an international alumni relations program, the university should determine why they want to engage international alumni and how to measure the program's benefits. Start with clear short-term and long-term objectives to support comprehensive internationalization. To help set these objectives, it is important to understand the university's international strategy to find ways international alumni can support it. For example, if the strategy calls to strengthen partner relationships and recruit students in a particular country, understanding international alumni demographics (where they live and work) can open many opportunities to support the strategy. Some short-term objectives to support student recruitment abroad can be to (1) start an international alumni program with specific target numbers of how many students will be recruited and (2) increase the number of engaged alumni in a particular country where international strategy calls to strengthen university partnerships or student recruitment.

Furthermore, learning how international alumni want to connect with the university is essential in establishing a two-way relationship; another short-term objective can be to survey all the international alumni in the institution's database or those in a particular country to better understand their own goals and motivations. The results can inform additional long-term objectives, such as building the number of international alumni chapters over time.

International alumni chapters also must have clear mission statements for why they exist, which should be aligned with the university's mission and goals. Therefore, alumni relations staff should clearly present chapters' connections to the university's mission, goals, and needs. This helps international alumni leadership and volunteers understand the larger picture they will be supporting. Working together with international alumni leaders in defining the chapter's mission and objectives allows them to develop ownership and embrace the benefits of joining, thus creating a win-win collaboration. For example, the chapter's mission can be to advance the university's reputation abroad while providing alumni with opportunities for professional networking, developing volunteer alumni leaders, and offering lifelong learning through the university's programs, academic staff, and distinguished alumni. (See figure 2 on page 25 for common strategic pillars.)

Leadership

Leadership is the second core component of building international alumni relations programs and chapters. Find and appoint enthusiastic alumni from different generations who understand the university's mission and needs and can commit their time and networks to help develop the chapter's own missions and objectives. To find enthusiastic alumni, search the institutional database for alumni who volunteered in student government, participated in student associations, received a scholarship, or are currently participating as university ambassadors. Those who were engaged during their studies and postgraduation are likely to be engaged alumni leaders as well.

Role descriptions for each of the alumni leaders, such as chair, secretary, treasurer, and communications expert, must be clear from the start. Role descriptions should include responsibilities and term limits, such as 1, 2, or 3 years for each appointed role; number of hours expected per month, quarter, or semester; and dates when international alumni leaders rotate out of their position. To facilitate continuity, it might be best to have half the international alumni leadership team rotate out in even years, while the others rotate in odd years.

Professional Staffing

Schools and universities developing international alumni programs and chapters require dedicated staff (part-time or full-time) who, when working abroad, can wear many hats, such as admissions, alumni relations, and development officers.

International alumni relations officers, as part of the institution's staff, can support alumni leaders. Today's international alumni relations officer is a global strategist at home and abroad. The role requires a variety of skills, such as interpersonal and intercultural communication, consensus-building, and project management expertise to work with constituencies from around the world. International alumni relations officers must also have the full support from institutional leadership for being on the front line, representing the institution in a variety of situations. Additionally, international alumni relations officers must have the stamina for regular travel and the energy to keep up with daily workload while on the road.

The opportunity to liaise with key international academic program leaders is also important for alumni relations officers, as they have direct access to international alumni who may want to host internships, sponsor holiday dinners for education abroad students in their city, and extend their own personal and professional networks to expand faculty research agendas.

Today, more campuses are focusing on international student recruitment, which creates another role for international alumni relations officers. By building relationships between new students, alumni chapters, and faculty from specific regions, the international alumni relations officer serves as a liaison for undergraduate and graduate students. Institutions that embrace hybrid roles or cross-training have an opportunity to enhance their employees' skills and international programs simultaneously.

Volunteer Management

Keeping track of international alumni volunteers and their contributions is another core component of international alumni relations programs. Rewarding volunteers helps with their retention and maintains their goodwill. Thanking them often is a low-cost way to improve volunteer relations. Here are some suggested ways to recognize and reward international alumni leaders:

- List alumni leaders' names and roles on the university's alumni website, annual newsletter, invitations, and event programs.
- Publicly acknowledge and thank them for their contributions at events (and do so privately as well).
- Send them an official thank-you letter or email after events and an accompanying certificate at the end of their volunteer term, along with small tokens of appreciation for their service.
- If possible, host an annual in-person or virtual party for all active volunteers and include an award for volunteer of the year. This event can be done per alumni chapter or for all chapters that are in close time zones.
- Create other volunteer awards to recognize alumni who have supported a program's success.

For more on recognition, see chapter 3.

Financial Planning

Finally, financial resources are one of the most important components of an international alumni relations program. The funds devoted to international alumni relations can impact strategy, the prospects for engaging alumni volunteers, the ability to initiate programs abroad, and the level of flexibility built into a program so that international alumni are prepared to respond to last-minute opportunities. Resources are finite and must be clearly identified and well managed.

One primary element of financial planning is developing an annual budget that aligns with the institution's fiscal calendar. Budgets for international alumni programs may be central or shared. A central budget is developed and managed by the designated full-time or part-time international alumni relations officer in conjunction with programmatic, communications, administrative, and other line item areas that compose one budget for alumni relations. The alumni relations budget is often part of a larger advancement division budget at the institution. A shared budget is developed by the designated international alumni relations officer and other key international education officers who engage (or have the potential to engage) alumni abroad. A shared budget can be created to support multiple agendas and events involving alumni, such as international student send-offs, international internships, and official visits by institutional leaders to build alumni relationships, develop academic partnerships, and showcase faculty talent.

Budgets for international alumni relations may also be supplemented through external partnerships with peer institutions, alumni, and families that lead to cosponsorship (two or more entities sponsoring an alumni network, professional development event, or major speaker in an international city). International alumni relations budgets may also be augmented by gifts in kind (the charitable donation of goods and services, as opposed to a direct donation of money to buy goods and services). In-kind support can come in the form of

- venue space (e.g., home country consulates and embassies);
- catering for meetings or events;
- production of printed promotional material and signage for international events;
- international student recruitment;
- professional services, such as videographers and hospitality; and
- local transfers when traveling abroad (e.g., families offering their personal car services).

International alumni relations officers should review their policies for accepting in-kind support from alumni, families, and other partners to ensure compliance with university policies.

University Support to International Alumni Chapters

Once the foundational components of an international alumni program are set in place, international alumni management and retention requires much support from the university. There are three common services and resources universities provide their chapters' international alumni leaders: database management, onboarding materials, and event and club promotion.

Database Management

Adding and updating international alumni contact details is essential to maintain the university's alumni database. Most universities have a landing page on their main website where alumni can add their personal and professional details or update their information. International alumni chapters can help send reminders to their members to update their info on the university's website. It is important that alumni chapters support the main university database rather than create their own spreadsheet or database to remain in compliance with any privacy laws and data-sharing regulations. Data regulations and protocols are increasingly being updated in various countries and regions around the world, and universities are required to remain in compliance with these protocols—a prominent example being the General Data Protection Regulation (GDPR) in the European Union.

Onboarding Materials

Many universities prepare a document providing volunteers with guidelines on how to start a chapter. It usually includes descriptions of the roles of leaders and how to recruit other volunteers and increase membership. For example, Brown University's Alumni Association (n.d.) offers a 25-page *Club Leader Toolkit*, consisting of clear instructions and tips on (1) the development of a club's mission statement; (2) how to start small, medium, and large clubs; (3) recommended yearly timelines; (4) sample club events; (5) communications; (6) administrative resources; and (7) finances and funding.

Event and Club Promotion

The university can help promote chapter events through its website and social media channels. It can also help clubs create newsletters and event announcements (with templates) and distribute them through the university alumni system. This ensures the most current alumni list is being used and adheres to opt-in/opt-out preferences in the customer relationship management (CRM) system and to data security protocols. The university can further offer website domain space and club listservs, which can be used to send the information and announcements. Some clubs may operate more independently by using approved tech platforms, but the data management must be in collaboration with the university.

Mapping Internal and External Stakeholders

Fundamental to successfully establishing and sustaining international alumni programs and chapters is support from internal and external stakeholders. This section identifies potential allies and the roles they can play in international alumni relations programs.

Internal Stakeholders

Mapping internal stakeholders and defining win-win collaborations can build buy-in for developing an international alumni relations program. For example, if operating the international alumni relations program from within the international office, collaborating with the alumni and fundraising office is indispensable, as is teaming up with the marketing and recruitment office, social media experts, the career office, and academic staff. To garner buy-in among top management (e.g., deans and heads of departments) and administrative staff, listen to these units' needs and provide answers to how they can benefit from an international alumni relations program. Keep departments and other internal stakeholders informed of how the international alumni relations program support their goals and the university as a whole. Figure 3 captures possible internal stakeholders from the perspective of the alumni relations office or international office, depending on where the international alumni relations program is housed. As the international alumni relations program grows, more internal stakeholders can be added.

Figure 3. Map of Internal Stakeholders

Chapter 2

External Stakeholders

Mapping external stakeholders helps identify who to count on in a strategic country or region. This mapping process might require some research and strong collaboration with the international, marketing, and recruitment offices and academic staff. For example, if there is a large group of alumni in China, list partner universities in China, organizations in the public and private sectors in China that are connected to the university through research collaborations, embassies, and any other stakeholder groups representing the university and country. Figure 4 provides an example of relevant external stakeholders abroad and in the home country who can support an international alumni relations program. The rightmost column includes examples of potential stakeholders on whom universities should keep an eye for long-term vision realization and investment. These future stakeholders might be engaged as the program evolves.

Figure 4. Map of External Stakeholders

Mapping external stakeholders provides an overview of the relationships that can be developed, activated, and sustained to strengthen international alumni engagement.

Return on Investment

Sometimes university leadership considers international alumni relations costly and difficult to measure in terms of return on investment (ROI). Therefore, to gain institutional buy-in and justify the costs, determine key performance indicators (KPIs) at the start of the program. KPIs must be aligned with the university's strategic goals and its international strategy. How does a particular activity help achieve an institutional strategic goal? The answer to this question will help create more effective activities. To determine what constitutes a successful alumni program, the 2016 *International CASE Alumni Relations Survey* (*ICARS*) measures three indicators of success—attendees, volunteers, and donors—and uses 27 variables to examine their degrees of correlation (CASE 2016). These variables include constituent databases, programs, resources, communications, events, and member benefits. The survey's results show that staff and budget are positively correlated with number of attendees and volunteers. Therefore, alumni relations programs with more resources can support more events and engage more volunteers. In addition, staff and budget are positively correlated with donors.

Furthermore, of the 84 participating universities in the survey, 94 percent offer alumni volunteer opportunities. Most of their alumni are primarily engaged in student recruitment, mentoring, and student employability. The *ICARS* report states the following recommendations (CASE 2016, 10):

1. **Stewardship:** To increase the number of attendees, instead of increasing the size of existing events, you need to have sufficient staff and budget to put on more events and be able to connect with potential attendees via email and e-newsletters.
2. **Ongoing contact:** To increase the number of volunteers, you need to be able to connect with them via e-newsletters, magazines, and professional development events.
3. **Engagement opportunities:** To increase the number of donors, you need to have the staff and budget to offer relevant programs and events that allow you to engage the constituents regularly.

Another helpful resource is the *Alumni Engagement Metrics* survey, published by CASE in 2020, which enables CASE member institutions to measure alumni engagement across four modes: philanthropic, volunteer, experiential, and communications. Although not specifically for international alumni engagement, this tool offers metrics on alumni engagement that can be used as starting points.

KPIs can be measured over time to compare growth over the years in relation to the number of staff and activities. Make sure they focus more on outcomes rather than outputs. In other words, although number of events, number of attendees, and volunteers (outputs) need to be measured, they should not be the only factors to measure a successful program. Outcomes-focused KPIs can indicate whether events and other activities instilled a greater sense of pride, connection, and ambassadorship from alumni. Define KPIs with international alumni leaders; do not provide them top-down. This way, international alumni leaders are part of the process and can take ownership of the chapter's goals and objectives.

In times of crisis or critical changes within an institution, goals should be adapted to the situation. If staff and budget have been reduced, review the KPIs to adjust priorities to meet goals and consider other modes of funding, such as joining forces with other departments, universities, or organizations.

A Case Study in International Alumni Program Development

KU Leuven, a research university in Belgium, provides a clear example of how a university has aligned leadership, faculty, and staff to set up an all-inclusive international alumni relations program and alumni chapters abroad. KU Leuven has interwoven its international alumni strategy with comprehensive internationalization to support the university's vision for a sustainable society. This case study puts into practice the components of international alumni relations programs discussed throughout the chapter, portraying a real-life example of these features in action.

CASE STUDY

Embedding International Alumni Relations in Internationalization Strategy: KU Leuven

By Martine Torfs, MA

Institution	KU Leuven
Motto	*Sedes Sapientiae* (Seat of wisdom)
Founded	1425
Location	Leuven, Belgium
Number of Students in 2020	59,000 students (16% of which are international)
Number of Alumni in 2020	282,000 (10% of which are international)

Department Responsible for International Alumni Relations	Fundraising and Alumni Relations Office
Alumni Relations Office Website	https://alum.kuleuven.be/eng

University Strategy

Founded in 1425, KU Leuven is a comprehensive university with 15 schools, offering 49 undergraduate and 142 graduate programs to 59,000 students and 282,000 alumni, who represent 170 nationalities. Identified as Europe's most innovative university for 4 years in a row (Reuters Staff 2019), KU Leuven's educational and research endeavors are spread over 13 campuses throughout the Belgian region of Flanders, with its main campus in Leuven. Its strategic plan, titled "On Crossroads, for a Sustainable Society," defines the common goals of education, research, and public outreach. The university's mission and core initiatives are intrinsically permeated by international perspectives.

Comprehensive Internationalization Strategy

KU Leuven's comprehensive internationalization strategy, titled Truly International, is geared to transition KU Leuven from a national university with a global reputation to a full-fledged international university (KU Leuven 2018). Institution-wide objectives include recruiting more and better qualified international students, improving the brand awareness of the university, increasing international collaboration opportunities for education and research, and enhancing specific programs to include partners in the Global South. As founding partner of the Una Europa Alliance, an alliance of eight European research universities drawing on their collective strengths to create a European inter-university environment, KU Leuven commits to comprehensive internationalization by engaging not only with partners but also with its alumni communities worldwide.

Alumni's Active Role in Internationalization

Internationalization efforts continually resulted in large numbers of engaged international alumni, including former international exchange students and visiting scholars. Acknowledging the value of this network, in 2011 the Alumni Relations Office started maintaining a database of KU Leuven's alumni and using CRM software jointly with its many traditional alumni associations based in Belgium. A budget was first allocated to support international alumni chapters in 2015 along with one part-time staff member. In 2018, the new Alumni Relations Strategy recognized alumni relations at the core of a comprehensive global stakeholder engagement approach.

"Alumni chapters are an important asset for KU Leuven," said Peter Lievens, vice rector for international and alumni policy, in 2019 during the launch in Beijing of KU Leuven's thirteenth international alumni chapter. "As more KU Leuven alumni go on to build international careers, we strengthen our global network."

The Alumni Relations Strategy is built on both the needs of alumni and the ambitions of the university. The international alumni support one another in their careers, while at the same time setting up coordinated programs in three fields:

1. **Branding and identity**
   - Enhance the brand and visibility of the university.
   - Keep alumni chapters attractive, visible, and active.
   - Set up innovative partnerships for research and education.
   - Develop a network of companies and corporate relations.
2. **Recruitment and career support**
   - Increase international student recruitment at KU Leuven.
   - Advance student and alumni employability.
   - Identify and facilitate opportunities for student and alumni training.
   - Facilitate access to the professional community for newcomers.
3. **Fundraising and philanthropy**
   - Advocate for KU Leuven's research, education, and heritage projects by asking others within their networks to donate or help fundraise.
   - Engage personally in philanthropy and donate.

Institutional Support

International alumni chapters act as local hubs of KU Leuven abroad and are meant to maintain a feeling of belonging, as they enable interactions between the alumni and the university. International alumni chapters as a rule do not charge membership fees but are volunteer-driven interfaces between alumni and KU Leuven through events and communications. The first international alumni chapters were set up between 2012 and 2016; during this pioneering phase, KU Leuven developed a support system, including budgets for events. The Alumni Office supports international alumni chapters to make an annual work plan and plays a role in organizing events, such as by helping find speakers, inviting stakeholders, and providing financial support to fill gaps if needed.

The recently incorporated digital alumni platform called KU Leuven Connect has been pivotal in engaging with alumni worldwide. It is a one-stop shop for alumni to liaise with the university (and vice versa) and with one another. Moreover, as a result of the COVID-19 pandemic, the Alumni Relations Office has provided a webinar tool to the alumni chapters for their events.

How International Alumni Chapters Are Embedded in the Organizational Structure

The success of alumni relations at KU Leuven is anchored in a university-wide collaboration structure of regional committees that match academic expertise with the relevant offices: academics and administrators in internationalization, alumni relations, and marketing and communications, with indirect links to admissions, fundraising, education, and research. The regional committees are firmly institutionalized, thus creating joint ownership of goals. A total of 5 regional committees are fully operational in an advisory role to the university's Council on International Policy, which reports directly to the university board. They consist of 6 to 10 expert members, bringing together a unique set of skills focused on one geographical area. One of the regional committee's experts represents the Alumni Relations Office, ensuring that alumni engagement programs are supported and identifying opportunities for collaboration. An alum, hired as a local part-time liaison officer for the university, serves as a member both of the regional committee and of the local alumni chapter's steering committee. The liaison officer's responsibilities include the alumni network, international recruitment, institutional collaborations, and corporate relations. If there is not already an international alumni chapter, the liaison officer will ensure connection with the local alumni community and assist in setting one up.

Three Tiers of International Alumni Chapters

KU Leuven distinguishes three tiers of alumni networks (see table 1). Tier 1 includes the chapters that are firmly tied to a regional committee; they boast strong ties between the international alumni volunteers and the university, which include guidance and support from an international liaison officer. Expectations are high in advancing key areas of the university's international strategy, such as ambassadorship and visibility, student recruitment, and alumni career development.

International alumni chapters that were active before the setup of the regional committees belong in Tier 2. They receive the same type of support as those in Tier 1, but they do not have a member in a regional committee nor a liaison officer in place yet.

Tier 3 includes potential international alumni chapters. In some countries, international alumni are engaged through specific programs with the international office, the alumni office, ambassador programs for recruitment, alumni advisory boards for the Global South, or other units. These international alumni usually assist in reaching out to others in their region, and while all the pieces of an international alumni chapter are not yet in place, these international alumni may lay the groundwork.

All international alumni receive an individual account on the university's digital alumni platform, KU Leuven Connect. Moreover, international alumni chapters are empowered to manage the alumni in their chapter's group on the platform, which can be compared to a Facebook group. For the time being, no groups can be formed bottom-up; they all start in collaboration with the university.

Table 1. Three Tiers of International Alumni Chapters

	Tier 1	Tier 2	Tier 3
Alumni Volunteer Makeup	Active volunteers (steering committee)	Active volunteers (steering committee)	No international alumni chapter, but some international alumni contact points
Direct Link with University	Strategic guidance by regional committee	Strategic guidance by vice rector and alumni office (no regional committee)	Provisional contact with the alumni office (no regional committee)
Local Staff	Support by an international liaison officer	No support by an international liaison officer	No support by an international liaison officer

	Tier 1	Tier 2	Tier 3
Virtual Engagement	Group on KU Leuven Connect with chapter's brand	Group on KU Leuven Connect with chapter's brand	No group on KU Leuven Connect (but all alumni have access)
Support for Administration, Data Management, and Financial Grants	Support package and intranet access	Support package and intranet access	Provisional support package

The Value of Alumni Loyalty

As alumni are increasingly mobile, and may even complete their programs and degrees from a distance, the value of a worldwide alumni network associated with the university's brand is evident. At KU Leuven, university leadership, faculty, and staff work together to fully embed international alumni in its comprehensive internationalization strategy.

Nurturing alumni's loyalty as part of the university's strategy enables flexibility when facing a crisis. Alumni worldwide are ambassadors for both future and current students—for education, research, and societal impact. While KU Leuven continuously widens its international reach, agility is crucial in the wake of situations like the COVID-19 pandemic or any other crises that require an ever-evolving approach to the university's alumni relations. Thanks to KU Leuven's organizational approach, international alumni chapters are not autonomous entities, but stakeholder relations hubs cocreated by the university and alumni and embedded in the international policy's regional approach. International alumni now have a clear role in implementing the university's vision, "On Crossroads, for a Sustainable Society."

Conclusion

As shown in the KU Leuven example, developing a successful international alumni relations program and chapters abroad demands a strategy that aligns with the university's comprehensive internationalization plan. It builds on university leadership as well as other internal and external stakeholders' endorsements and support. An effective strategy requires clear definitions of target groups, goals, metrics, and long-term financial investments. But above all, it needs to incorporate its international alumni as strategic partners willing to advise, liaise, lead, and contribute in expanding their alma mater's vision and mission abroad.

References

billhighway and Mariner Management & Marketing. 2019. *Chapter Benchmarking Report: Data, Success Stories & Opinions.* https://marinermanagement.com/wp-content/uploads/2019/10/2019_Chapter_Benchmarking_Report_Final.pdf.

Brown University Alumni Association. n.d. *Club Leader Toolkit.* http://advancement.brown.edu/brunonia/docs/Club_Leader_Toolkit.pdf.

Council for Advancement and Support of Education (CASE). 2016. *Engaging for Excellence: Alumni Relations Programmes in European Higher Education: ICARS Report 2016.* London, UK: CASE. https://www.case.org/system/files/media/file/ICARS_Report_2015_v2.pdf.

Council for Advancement and Support of Education (CASE). 2020. *CASE Global Alumni Engagement Metrics Survey.* August 31. https://www.case.org/resources/case-global-alumni-engagement-metrics-survey.

Dobson, Gretchen, ed. 2015. *Staying Global: How International Alumni Relations Advances the Agenda.* EAIE Occasional Paper 24.

KU Leuven. 2018. "Strategic Plan for KU Leuven in 5 Projects." https://www.kuleuven.be/english/about-kuleuven/strategic-plan/truly-international.

Reuters. 2019. "Reuters Top 100: Europe's Most Innovative Universities 2019 Announced." *Reuters PR* (blog). April 30. https://www.reuters.com/article/rpbtop1002019/reuters-top-100-europes-most-innovative-universities-2019-announced-idUSKCN1S60PA.

Samuels, Lavern. 2020. Interview by Sandra Rincón. August 7, 2020.

Una Europa. 2020. "Making the University of the Future a Reality." https://una-europa.imgix.net/documents/Press-Release-1Europe-Kick-off.pdf.

Chapter 3

A Framework for Growing and Maintaining International Alumni Engagement

The Council for Advancement and Support of Education (CASE), the organization for advancement professionals who work in alumni relations, defines alumni engagement as "activities that are valued by alumni, build enduring and mutually beneficial relationships, inspire loyalty and financial support, strengthen the institution's reputation, and involve alumni in meaningful activities to advance the institution's mission" (CASE 2018, 5). In this book, international alumni engagement extends CASE's description by specifying that the activities mentioned above can take place anywhere to guide international alumni in inspiring goodwill, nurturing cross-cultural understanding, and advancing the institution's global impact. While chapter 2 explored how to establish international alumni programs at an institutional level, this chapter concentrates on engaging international alumni on the individual level. The chapter starts by looking into why engaging international students from the start precedes an international alumni program. Then, a detailed description of the LEARN Model for International Alumni Relations provides a guiding framework and toolkit to help establish, manage, and evaluate an international alumni relations program. The chapter concludes with two case studies from the field: (1) "How to Create Content That Will Resonate with Online Communities" argues that content should be well planned, as it is essential for growing and maintaining healthy online alumni communities; (2) "Alumni Awards: Multiplying Reach and Impact" shares how alumni awards, as part of the Study UK campaign, celebrate international alumni's outstanding achievements.

Chapter 3

Fostering International Student Engagement First

The relationship with international alumni starts early on when these individuals are still prospective students. When looking for an educational program, international students are usually advised by family members, friends, alumni, and agents or through the information found on the internet. Once prospective students contact the university, how well recruiters and admissions officers respond to their inquiries and needs signals how much the university values them. When they find international alumni testimonials that personify the educational experience, it transmits a shared experience. Offering an international alumni chapter in prospective students' home countries or global networks could convey the university's investment in providing valuable support networks and resources for students and alumni. Some universities now include the benefits of the institution's alumni networks in their promotional materials, videos, and websites when informing prospective students about their academic programs.

The arrival phase of the international student life cycle is likely one of the most memorable stages of students' experiences abroad. Providing a smooth arrival during which students can easily find housing, have opportunities to make friends with local students, and meet international alumni who have stayed to work in the host country helps students feel welcome in their new academic and social communities. This welcoming environment should continue throughout the students' time on campus. As they prepare to graduate, do international students leave with a sense of pride and belonging to an academic and student-alumni community? Do they understand their roles as alumni, and will they be engaged alumni? When universities and their schools align their goals with ongoing support and engagement throughout the international students' time on campus, memorable and engaging experiences will continue to resonate throughout their international alumni journeys.

Institutional support plays an important role in international students' success in the host university and country. Thus, collective efforts of faculty and staff who provide programs and services that foster engagement with other students and the campus community constitute a large part of the international student-alumni journey. International students often have far fewer resources for educational, social, and cultural adjustment in the host university and society. A study on the roles of university support for international students in U.S. universities shows that "while university support increased international students' school-life satisfaction, it reduced their psychological stress" (Cho and Yu 2015, 21). When students move across countries to study and experience new ways of life, the institution becomes their home and classmates become their family. The university that welcomes and provides on-campus support and a sense of community will generate loyal and engaged international alumni.

International Student-Alumni Journey

Figure 1 exemplifies the international student-alumni journey. It shows the main touch points of students' experiences in the process of becoming engaged alumni. It also includes the different administrative offices, academic units, and international alumni chapters that can work together in each phase.

Figure 1. Touch Points and Service Offices

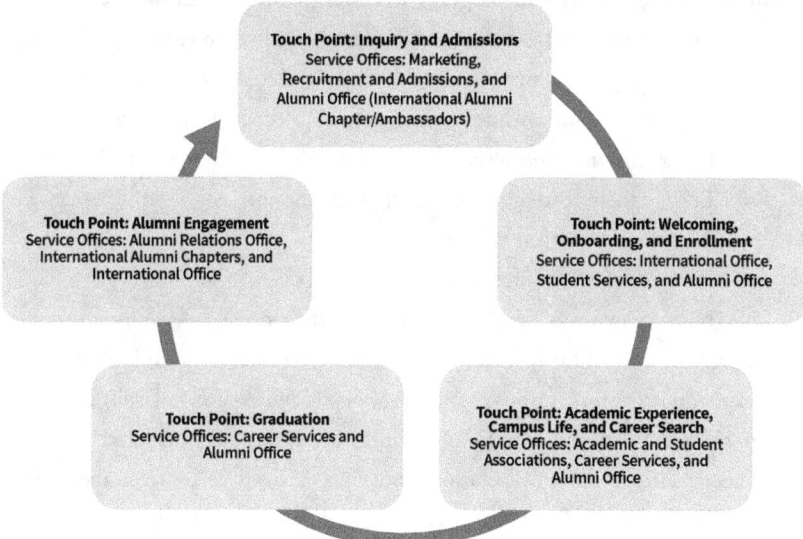

Reflecting on the experience to be delivered in each phase helps universities ensure international students' engagement. Some questions to consider: Does each administrative office provide services in silo, or is there an integrated, institution-wide approach? Does each phase support the others in delivering a common message and memorable experience? Is there a common story that transmits the university's core values?

Research from the business sector may shed light on how to create a memorable international student experience. A study across hundreds of corporate brands indicates that "the most effective way to maximize value is to move beyond mere customer satisfaction and connect with customers at an emotional level" (Zorfas and Leemon 2016, 2). This study listed 10 strong emotional motivators, such as the desires to feel a sense of belonging, succeed in life, and feel secure. International educators know that these emotional motivators resonate with many students who studied abroad. A college experience needs to include these emotional motivators when building the international student-alumni journey.

LEARN Model for International Alumni Relations

I (Sandra) was introduced to the LEARN Model for Alumni Relations at the CASE European Conference in August 2009,[1] just as I was starting to develop an international alumni relations program at Tilburg University in the Netherlands. I adapted this framework to international alumni relations to create a toolkit that can be used to establish, manage, and evaluate international alumni relations programs. LEARN stands for Locate, Engage, Ask, Recognize, and Nurture:

Locate international alumni.

Engage them through intentional programming.

Ask them to serve as volunteers.

Recognize their contributions and successes.

Nurture two-way relationships to meet their needs.

The LEARN Model for International Alumni Relations is a guiding framework for higher education institutions to engage, evaluate, and expand mutually beneficial relationships with their international alumni. It requires an integrated approach that incorporates close collaboration with internal and external stakeholders. Figure 2 shows the LEARN Model as a continual five-phase process. It is followed by descriptions of each phase and actionable checklists for implementing the phase in any institutional context.

Figure 2. LEARN Model

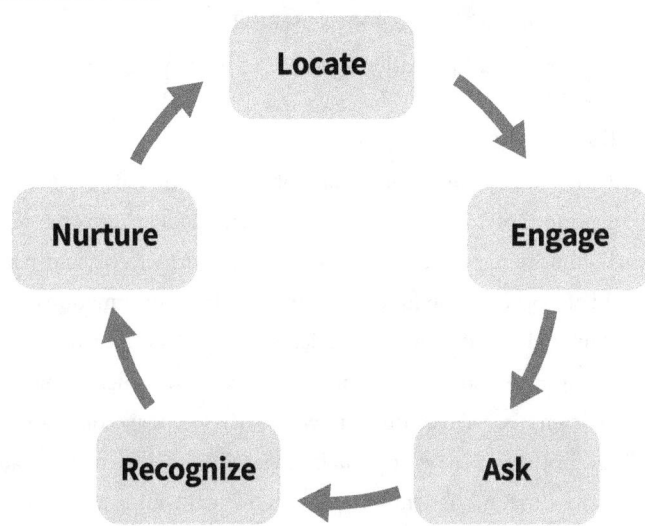

Locate

Identifying and locating international alumni constitutes the foundation of any program or chapter. Customer relationship management (CRM) software that specializes in alumni relations and fundraising is essential in building international alumni relations programs. Collecting data of alumni living abroad is difficult and requires the institutional legal department's advice on what information can be collected and saved. For many, the best place to start is by gathering students' data before graduation. The form that students fill out to confirm they have met all the requirements before graduation can include a request to provide their personal email addresses. A disclaimer stating what the university will do with alumni's data, developed with the legal department, needs to be included.

Some universities locate their alumni abroad by running social media campaigns requesting alumni register directly to the university's database. LinkedIn offers alumni listings within the university page. It allows almost any university around the world to easily locate its alumni by showing the number of alumni (those who included the university on their profile), where they live (by country and city), where they work (name of the company), and what they do (field of work). In its listings, LinkedIn includes students, former exchange students, and those who completed a certificate or degree. LinkedIn is a useful tool to gain a quick overview of alumni who could be contacted in a particular country and city. Who to include as alumni in an institution's database depends on the definition of alumni and the goals and objectives of the international alumni relations program (see chapter 2).

Data Collection

Apart from basic data (name, gender, date of birth, nationality, study program, degree, graduation year), collect other information that can be useful for international alumni engagement, such as alumni's current city and country of residence, field of work, and job function. Other pertinent information can include whether an alum had a study abroad experience, was a board member of a student association, received a scholarship from the university or other organization, or volunteered at campus events. Students who actively engage on campus while enrolled at the institution tend to remain engaged with their alma mater once they graduate. Research on philanthropy shows that cultivating a culture of giving should start on campus through volunteering or small donations (Gallo 2013). Therefore, keeping track of international student volunteers can help build a base of international alumni volunteers and donors who, for example, can help build alumni communities abroad or fundraise for international student scholarships.

Checklist to Locate
- ✓ Ensure all collected data can be stored in CRM software, and follow the data protection regulations of the host country.
- ✓ Reach out to student services and alumni relations offices for a list of current international students and international alumni. Focus on country of origin, as students and graduates often remain mobile but still stay connected to their home country.
- ✓ Check with the international office for lists of former and current exchange students (incoming and outgoing).
- ✓ Run social media campaigns asking alumni to update their data.
- ✓ Use LinkedIn for quick overviews of alumni's locations, job sectors, and companies where they work.
- ✓ Map internal and external stakeholders (see chapter 2). Prioritize them according to the university's international strategy.
- ✓ Collaborate with career services, marketing and recruitment, and the international office to track international alumni who have attended recent events in person or virtually.

Engage

Once international alumni have been located, learning how they want to be engaged is essential in establishing a two-way relationship. Social media facilitates engagement with a large section of international alumni populations. Use any chosen medium to foster two-way communications rather than only sending out information. Allow international alumni to have a voice by commenting or sharing experiences.

There are many ways to engage alumni through social media, events, and community building. Deciding how to develop a sound engagement plan requires intention, staff, budget, and time. An engagement plan must be aligned with the objectives of the international alumni relations program and how it advances internationalization. Thus, to draft an engagement plan that meets these objectives, close collaboration between the alumni office and the international office is necessary. Who is ultimately responsible for creating and implementing the engagement plan depends on whether the international alumni relations program will be under the supervision of the alumni office or the international office.

Start with a short survey asking international alumni how they would like to be involved with their alma mater, what type of information they would like to receive, and how they would like to stay informed. Figure 3 provides a list of questions for surveying international alumni and potential responses. Research shows that long surveys discourage participant completion (Galesic and Bosnjak 2009). Therefore, think through the type of information needed to craft concise surveys to best capture how international alumni want to be engaged.

Figure 3. International Alumni Survey Questions

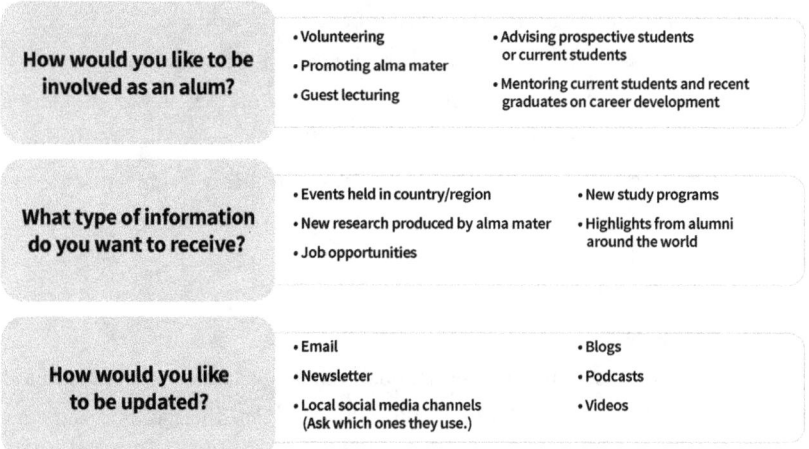

Segmented Engagement

How and what to communicate to international students and alumni to foster a mutually beneficial engagement depends on whether they just arrived on campus, are about to graduate, are starting their careers, or are well established in their professions. Therefore, segment student and alumni groups by interests and phases in their lives. In marketing communications, segmentation divides the database into groups of individuals who are similar in specific ways. Segmented groups can be determined by similarities such as personal characteristics (age, graduation year, country of residence), preferences (study program, social media channels), or behaviors (volunteer activity, sports, clubs). Consider the following international student-alumni phases in figure 4 to help segment students and alumni during their life cycle.

Figure 4. International Student-Alumni Phases

Prospective students	Current students	New alumni looking to start their careers	Alumni looking to advance their careers	Well-established alumni willing to help others

Segmentation helps institutions allocate resources and time for engaging alumni more effectively by meeting groups' needs and preferences. For example, experienced alumni will be less interested in job opportunities than recent graduates, but they might be willing to mentor, offer internships to students or recent graduates, help fundraise, or donate money to a scholarship fund. Alternately, for many international students, getting help with finding an internship and learning to navigate the local labor market are essential functions that alumni can help fulfill. Institutions can coordinate these mutually beneficial relationships and help all segmented groups engage in meaningful experiences and relationships.

Communication and engagement plans for each of the phases should be developed and aligned with the overall goals and objectives of the international alumni relations program. To develop these plans, consider working with internal stakeholders, such as student services, the international office, the career office, and other campus units.

Online Engagement

Universities with established international alumni relations programs have been engaging international alumni online for a while. These online activities have included board meetings with international chapter leaders, professional development webinars, forums, blogs, and newsletters. Online events also include conferences, workshops, coffee break sessions, and graduation ceremonies. These activities use software to poll, facilitate brainstorming, break out into group discussions, and network.

Recently, many online events have attracted more alumni since in-person events were either not available in their city, too expensive to attend, or impractical to travel to. For example, Erasmus Mundus Alumni Association's (EMA) first online General Assembly (GA) kicked off in 2020 with the theme "EMA Changemakers for Global Solidarity." Nearly 300 international alumni from different countries and time zones around the world participated in the GA, which normally attracts around 50 members (Imani 2020). Brown University's "Virtual Engagement Toolkit"—a CASE gold award winner—offers its alumni volunteers clear guidance on organizing their own social media engagement, virtual events, and email communication (Brown Alumni & Friends n.d.). As Andrew Shaindlin (2021), vice president for alumni relations at Brown University, says:

> Because of the [COVID-19] pandemic, and the dramatic shift we had to make to fully online interaction, the best thing we have provided volunteers (not just in Clubs) is our Virtual Engagement Toolkit. It allows volunteer alumni at all levels of time commitment and availability to maintain connections with other alumni. And it works for different kinds of audience segments—class year, regional club, cultural or ethnic and racial affinity; professional shared interest, etc.

Checklist to Engage

Communication Plan

- ✓ Survey international alumni on the type of information they want to receive and how.
- ✓ Develop a plan to keep international alumni informed of what is happening at the university and its impact on global society.
- ✓ Nurture pride and nostalgia for the time international alumni spent on campus. Use photographs, short videos, and back-to-campus events.
- ✓ Foster lifelong learning; communicate about new online programs, webinars, and podcasts.

- ✓ Share stories about alumni (alumni who fell in love on campus, have made a societal impact, reinvented their careers, etc.). Alumni want to know about each other; use content to inspire them!

Events
- ✓ Organize alumni reunions in strategic countries where the institution has student and staff exchanges, internships, research collaborations, recruitment activities, active alumni, or a large number of international alumni who are not yet engaged.
- ✓ Collaborate with the international, alumni engagement, and career offices as well as student associations to bring awareness to how international alumni and international alumni chapters can benefit students during their time on campus and after graduation. When possible, include external stakeholders in events in strategic countries.
- ✓ Develop event content based on international alumni interests. When possible, include prospective and current international students.
- ✓ Offer virtual events for international alumni communities.
- ✓ Work with the university's international student associations and clubs. If they do not exist, help create one to start engaging international students.

Tools
- ✓ Research which social media platforms international students and alumni commonly use in their home countries.
- ✓ Select alumni relations software that meets the needs of both the institution and alumni. (Many alumni software companies offer platforms for institutions to own the data collected.)
- ✓ Remember that content, not the tool, is what drives online engagement.

Record
- ✓ Keep track of how activities serve the international alumni program's objectives.
- ✓ Mark in the database alumni who donate their time, expertise, and money; organize events; offer internships and jobs; or play any other key role. These alumni can become champion (or "ambassador") alumni to help bring others on board.
- ✓ Note alumni who attend events or are popular social media leaders. These international alumni can bring others on board by helping to organize programming and lead social media campaigns in their home countries.

Ask

Two-way engagement needs to be established before asking alumni to give back to their alma mater. The ask comes after defining how the institution can still be relevant and supportive of its international alumni. When the university reaches out to international alumni, either to invite them to an event, provide a testimonial, or give advice, the alumni normally feel honored and are happy to contribute. Institutions can create a short survey for all international alumni or a group in a particular country or region that asks respondents if they would like to volunteer for a specific activity or in general. This topic can be added to the survey on the type of information alumni want to receive (see figure 3).

International alumni can give back in different ways during their alumni life span. Be clear as to what the university needs in order to advance internationalization and how alumni can help meet the program's goals. Some examples can be to help raise funds for scholarships for international students, welcome new outgoing exchange students in their home country, recruit new international students, advise prospective students through the admissions process, or help sponsor or look for sponsors for an event. Keep alumni informed of how their contribution makes a difference for the university, students, and their international community.

When asking international alumni to volunteer their time or services, describe their roles, responsibilities, tasks, and goals they should meet. Include in the description the amount of time they are expected to volunteer and to whom they will report. Set up short training sessions online and have regular meetings with them to answer any questions. (For more on training, see chapter 4.) Remember that they have other commitments and their time is valuable, so use it effectively. Make sure to have a two-way evaluation once volunteers have completed their tasks. Ask them how they would like to volunteer in the future or offer them a way to continue their involvement.

Checklist to Ask

- ✓ Develop a survey to identify international alumni who can be asked to volunteer, provide internships, and mentor current international students and new alumni.
- ✓ Establish international alumni chapters abroad to maintain a constant pool of volunteers who can be asked to support the institution's branding, recruitment, and culture and knowledge exchange.

- ✓ Grow and maintain a circle of prominent alumni abroad who can be asked to facilitate business contacts or international fundraising. Many international alumni can provide information about new scholarship funding available from public or private sectors and companies that can sponsor an event or support an international student scholarship fund.
- ✓ Ask international alumni to share testimonials and stories for the university's website and social media.
- ✓ Note that international alumni volunteers should be well instructed and trained on what they are asked to perform and deliver.

Recognize

"How well a university shows its alumni how much they matter to the university determines the degree of connectedness to their institution" (Conroy and Rincón 2012, 31). Recognize international alumni efforts and successes to show the university's pride in their accomplishments. Remember that international alumni's success in their careers and social impact contribute to the development and expansion of the university's global reputation and service mission. Establish international alumni spotlights to highlight alumni's stories of professional accomplishment. Recognize international alumni who hold high positions in their fields, do humanitarian work, have a positive social impact, and are innovators or entrepreneurs; publish their stories to inspire others. Scholarships awarded to international students should be publicized throughout the international alumni community, including with parents. Some universities award prizes for best master's thesis and PhD dissertation during graduation ceremonies. Communicate about these awards and create a spotlight story around each. This nurtures pride among international alumni communities, keeps international alumni informed of current students' accomplishments, and recognizes the students for these achievements.

It is particularly important to also recognize accomplishments related to international alumni's roles with their alma mater. Create awards for the most engaged international alumni volunteer or group of volunteers, such as alumni board members of an international chapter. Here are some examples:

1. **Volunteer Award:** international alumni who have donated their time and expertise as board members of international clubs or chapters, brand ambassadors, keynote speakers for alumni events, and mentors for career development. The institution might send them a thank-you card for their contribution, for example.

2. **Graduated with Merit Award:** international alumni who have received prizes, scholarships, or research grants. These alumni can be in a spotlight on the university website and alumni newsletter or magazine.
3. **Career Achievement Award:** international alumni who make a positive social impact or have high positions in their professional field. This category requires more research in the institution's database, provided international alumni are updating their information, or through LinkedIn. International alumni chapters and country embassies abroad can facilitate the search for prominent alumni in strategic countries.

Checklist to Recognize
- ✓ Implement a plan to recognize international alumni who volunteered, graduated with merit, or made an achievement in their career.
- ✓ Inform the larger university and alumni communities about international alumni achievements.
- ✓ Convey appreciation for international alumni both publicly and privately.
- ✓ Keep track of alumni's noteworthy achievements and contributions to create newsletters or other recognition materials more easily.

Nurture

Nurturing a two-way relationship—a recurring theme throughout all stages of the model—ensures international alumni continue to find value in their lifelong involvement, grow their engagement, and strengthen their relationship with their alma mater. International alumni have different needs throughout their lives (see figure 4). The needs of recent graduates are different from those of alumni who are further along in their careers. Most recent international graduates need to find a job quickly after completing their studies. Ways to nurture the two-way relationship and stay relevant to their needs include offering advice, internship options, mentors, and an alumni network. Alumni who have established careers might be looking for other opportunities to grow within their sector or change sectors; thus lifelong learning opportunities as well as professional and personal development workshops can nurture their engagement (see chapter 6).

As economies become more flexible and alumni more mobile, international networks are indispensable to meet alumni needs. Established alumni communities abroad can serve as home base for mobile alumni, connecting them with friends and helping them make new ones. As more international alumni work away from their home country, providing them with an international alumni community in person or online where they can share with others similar experiences of studying and working abroad helps nurture the two-way relationship with their alma mater and other alumni.

Checklist to Nurture
- ✓ Establish chapters, clubs, and communities of alumni abroad and develop activity plans with the international alumni volunteers to meet their needs and support the university.
- ✓ Establish virtual chapters and clubs by themes. This allows alumni to connect depending on their interests, rather than by location.
- ✓ Ensure chapters have sufficient staff support to nurture collaboration with alumni. Focus on building relationships with international alumni leaders and not on growing the number of clubs abroad. Building fewer, well-resourced communities can be more engaging, mutually enriching, and beneficial for all involved.

Conclusion

Building successful relationships with international alumni requires institutions to not only engage individuals after graduation but also as students. Reflecting on the experience delivered during the different phases of the international student-alumni cycle helps universities build two-way relationships as they incorporate the needs and interests of their students and alumni into their programs. The LEARN Model for International Alumni Relations offers a framework that guides institutions through the individual and group engagement to ensure sustainable, mutual benefits for both the institution and alumni.

Practices from the Field

This section shares two model practices from the field to emphasize important aspects of alumni engagement: delivering content and recognizing alumni's accomplishments. In the first example, Jean Hamon, CEO of Hivebrite, a software company dedicated to alumni management and engagement, shares how to develop and plan relevant content to engage an online community. In the second example, Huw Davies, campaign manager for Study UK, shares how the organization's alumni awards program has evolved, what the organization has learned in the process, and how both Study UK and the alumni have benefited.

CASE STUDY

How to Create Content That Resonates with Online Communities
By Jean Hamon, MBA

Organization	Hivebrite
Motto	Unlock the power of your community.
Primary Services	Alumni management, alumni engagement, fundraising, membership management, events, mentoring, and career services
Founded	2015
Locations	Global
Website and Social Media	- https://hivebrite.com - https://www.linkedin.com/company/hivebrite - https://twitter.com/hivebrite - https://www.facebook.com/hivebrite

Content is an essential ingredient for growing and maintaining a healthy online international alumni community. If an international alumni community is going to be successful, it needs a clear vision to build a robust content strategy. As the community grows, its vision should be communicated again and again. The right type of content will help engage and grow membership, build trust, and strengthen relationships.

Creating a Content Strategy

Why does a well-thought-out content strategy matter? To ensure the right type of content is delivered to the right group of alumni at the right time. Therefore, it is important to understand community members. What are their needs, interests, and pain points? Creating marketing personas is a useful technique to better understand the target audience. A marketing persona refers to the ideal customer for a particular business, brand, or service. Personas are defined by a mixture of any of the following attributes and activities: demographic, location, job function, interest in product or service, and need for the product or service. These attributes can all be used to create personas for international alumni groups.

Once marketing personas have been developed for each international alumni group, try to come up with three or four main content topics relevant to each group. Each content topic should be analyzed in terms of relevance and value to the community members. Consider also modes of communication (video, blogs, podcasts, etc.) and how each group prefers to receive the content (email, text notification, etc.).

Brand Voice: How to Talk to an Online Audience

Once the audience and the best way to reach them have been defined, the next step is to determine how to talk to the target groups. Using the language and style that each target audience understands is key to building a connection. One of the most common methods to define brand voice is based on the following four dimensions:

1. **Humor (funny vs. serious):** Does the content allow for a humorous tone? Or does it require a more serious approach?
2. **Formality (formal vs. casual):** Should the writing be formal or informal? For example, an older alumni audience might respond to a more formal approach.
3. **Enthusiasm (animated vs. matter-of-fact):** Will the tone of communication be enthusiastic or more subdued?
4. **Respectfulness:** Have the content creators considered the cultural norms of the audience to ensure they are not using an irreverent approach?

Ask stakeholders to weigh in on the first three dimensions above and evaluate the final text for the fourth. Stakeholders' feedback helps create the foundation for the community's brand voice. Whether it is funny or serious, formal or casual, animated or matter-of-fact, the community's brand voice should be defined from the start and remain consistent across all channels.

Organizing Content Creation

An ad-lib approach to content creation will not suffice in the long run. Producing quality, well-researched content takes time. A content calendar is key to planning and organizing future content. (Not to mention it spares the pressure of coming up with a topic right before a publication deadline.) A content calendar ensures

that communications stay consistent and on track. Are there special dates for the community (Earth Day, Giving Tuesday, Pride Day, International Women's Day, International Day of Peace, etc.)? Harness the buzz around dates that matter to the international community, and create a dedicated content campaign. A content calendar also makes it easy to spot gaps in content creation, to see if too much focus is given to one topic while neglecting another. Mapping out topics can also inspire other content ideas. A content calendar should include the following:
1. Content topics
2. Publication frequency (times per week, month, etc., content will be shared)
3. Publishing dates
4. Content distribution and promotion channels
5. The designated owner of each content piece or channel
6. Processes for validating content, plus a method for storing and sharing drafts

Online spreadsheets are great places to keep a content calendar. They allow multiple people to access and update the document in real time.

Measuring the Effectiveness of Content Creation

To know the value of the content created, it is important to evaluate it. The best way to evaluate content depends on the community's overall goals. Some examples of metrics include
1. email open rates;
2. post engagement;
3. online form completions; and
4. shares on social media.

Whatever the metrics, be sure to evaluate content efforts at least once a quarter.

Create Content That Gets the Community Excited

Get creative. Produce content that people will want to consume. Tell the community's story. Pack communications with passion. Experiment with different content formats and see what gets the best results from the target audience: bite-size videos, curated content, longer written content formats, or punchy Q&As.

Also, leverage user-generated content. Are international alumni discussing the latest event, sharing photos, and giving feedback? Repurpose this content into a blog post. Collaborating with the university's marketing brand platform and with the communications and marketing department can help to repurpose marketing material and ignite new content that serves both parties. All in all, the key to success lies in aligning every piece of content with the overall community strategy, as well as creating intentional messaging and a well-organized schedule.

CASE STUDY

Alumni Awards: Multiplying Reach and Impact
By Huw Davies

Business Name	British Council
Motto	The United Kingdom's international organization for cultural relations and educational opportunities
Primary Services	Arts and culture, education, and English language learning
Founded	1934
Location	Global
Website	https://www.britishcouncil.org/

The Study UK campaign was launched in 2016 by the British Council, in partnership with the UK government's GREAT Britain campaign, to promote the United Kingdom as a first-choice study destination internationally. The opportunities to promote their brands and grow their international alumni networks enticed institutions to partake in the campaign. The positive impact of the campaign to the UK economy to date, based on the value per international student per year, is £522 million.

As part of the overall Study UK strategy, the annual Alumni Awards program celebrates international UK university alumni, raising their profile as well as that of the United Kingdom as a study destination. There are three award categories for applicants: professional achievement, entrepreneurial, and social impact. In this international, digital campaign, 21 finalists' stories are showcased over several months, culminating in the three winners visiting the United Kingdom to boost their networks and careers. The primary goal of the Alumni Awards is to recognize

recipients' accomplishments and boost their job prospects in their home country. The Alumni Awards have evolved over time, revealing the following important lessons:
1. **Make it as easy as possible for stakeholders to engage with the campaign:** Provide a range of options for institutions, organizations, and participants to take part—for example, sharing the campaign logo and branding, which are free and easy for them to incorporate into their own content.
2. **Work in partnership:** Share plans with stakeholders (universities and sector bodies) and ensure all interests (e.g., raising UK universities' profile globally and growing universities' alumni networks) are met.
3. **Start small and build on solid foundations:** This awards program was started 6 years ago in three key markets (China, India, and the United States). By the third year, 12 countries were participating, and by the fourth year, alumni from 123 countries, representing more than 85 percent of UK higher education institutions, had applied. Although the Alumni Awards program is mainly geared toward alumni, the content that is generated feeds into student recruitment and builds brands internationally, both for the United Kingdom and the individual universities represented.

The Alumni Awards program has grown into an international awards program that has achieved excellent reach and impact. More information about the awards can be found at study-uk.britishcouncil.org/alumni-awards.

References

Brown Alumni & Friends. n.d. "Virtual Engagement Toolkit." Brown University. https://sites.google.com/brown.edu/virtualengagementtoolkit/home.

Cho, Jaehee, and Hongsik Yu. 2015. "Roles of University Support for International Students in the United States: Analysis of a Systematic Model of University Identification, University Support, and Psychological Well-Being." *Journal of Studies in International Education* 19, 1:11–27.

Conroy, Philip, and Sandra Rincón. 2012. "International Alumni Matters." *Forum*, Spring. https://www.eaie.org/our-resources/library/publication/Forum-Magazine/2012-spring-forum.html;jsessionid=A11A6B51F0700B4 6778666E279FD39B7.

Council for Advancement and Support of Education (CASE). 2018. *Engaging for Excellence: Generating Alumni Support for Higher Education 2018*. https://www.case.org/system/files/media/file/Engaging_for_excellence_2018_final.pdf.

Galesic, Merta, and Michael Bosnjak. 2009. "Effects of Questionnaire Length on Participation and Indicators of Response Quality in a Web Survey." *Public Opinion Quarterly* 73, 2:349–60.

Gallo, Maria L. 2013. "Higher Education Over a Lifespan: A Gown to Grave Assessment of a Lifelong Relationship Between Universities and Their Graduates." *Studies in Higher Education* 38, 8:1150–61.

Imani, Fatema. 2020. "EMA's General Assembly 2020 Gathered Members from All Over the World in a Large Video Conference on May 16th and 17th." Erasmus Mundus Association.

Shaindlin, Andrew. 2021. Interview by Sandra Rincón. February 8, 2021.

Study UK. 2021. "Alumni Awards." British Council. https://study-uk.britishcouncil.org/alumni-awards.

Zorfas, Alan, and Daniel Leemon. 2016. "An Emotional Connection Matters More than Customer Satisfaction." *Harvard Business Review.* August 29. https://hbr.org/2016/08/an-emotional-connection-matters-more-than-customer-satisfaction.

---

[1] Despite diligent research, the authors of this publication were unable to identify the creator(s) of this 2009 CASE presentation. Nevertheless, we thank them for their foundational framework and scholarship.

Chapter 4

International Alumni Ambassador Programs

International alumni ambassadors are key drivers of their alma mater's internationalization efforts. They are individual alumni or other key internal and external stakeholders who are deeply connected to the institution, personally and professionally, and influence the internationalization agenda for the institution. The difference between international alumni ambassadors and international alumni in general is that institutions consistently engage with ambassadors as they promote the institution's brand abroad. International alumni ambassador programs invest in long-term relationships with their members. Such programs can help build institutional reputation, recruit new international students, and bridge relationships with other institutions, organizations, or donors abroad.

Following descriptions of internal and external stakeholders who can serve as international ambassadors, this chapter offers suggestions for establishing and facilitating international alumni ambassador programs. It addresses how to train, recognize, and sustain individuals in these roles and assess a program's success. An essay by an international advancement consultant emphasizes strategies for assessing programs. Next, the chapter examines how international parents and family members add value as active international ambassadors, concluding with a case study of the University of Rochester's China Parent Network.

Internal and External Stakeholders as Ambassadors

All institutions can tap their international alumni as ambassadors to help advance their vision and strategy, but many still need to recognize that their international ambassador community extends to international students and internal and external stakeholders who can support internationalization in times of uncertainty. Ambassadors can also include leadership, faculty, staff, current students, families, and more. The following highly involved stakeholders are key allies for international alumni ambassador programs.

Internal Stakeholders

- **Leadership** sets the tone and inspires all other stakeholders to invest their time, talent, and treasure in upholding the international mission and activities of the institution.
- **Faculty** (often the university representatives who speak to international alumni audiences in person while promoting their research around the world) lead transnational, educational discussions and continue to wear the institutional banner as they participate in international conferences or collaborate on academic partnerships.
- **Staff** are increasingly active in advancing their institution's brand during virtual recruitment fairs, professional conferences, special events, and fundraising activities. Through asynchronous, remote, or in-person conversations, staff build greater brand recognition among prospective students and international partners.
- **Current students** communicate daily with prospective students about their experience via social media and peer-to-peer online portals. Prospective international students gain insights and knowledge from current students.

External Stakeholders

- **Families** of international students are truly VIP ambassadors, as they can network locally and serve as valuable marketing engines for institutions. Knowledgeable and engaged families extend the institution's international influence as it seeks to maintain or expand recruitment channels, connect local students and alumni with regional internships and new jobs, and provide offshore communities for other families. (See more on families as ambassadors later in the chapter.)
- **Transnational alumni** also inspire greater international engagement. Former international students who remained in (or returned after a period of time to) an institution's immediate community or region may be part of the transnational diaspora composed of alumni, families, faculty, and staff. Knowing these demographic details creates more opportunities to involve communities in conversations about international priorities at home and abroad.

- **Industry and governmental partners** can also provide guidance to an institution seeking to build and secure its reputation in new or existing markets. Alumni contacts in academia, local industries, or governmental positions are invaluable resources to an institution motivated to develop programs in other countries.

Investing in the International Alumni Ambassador Experience

A dedicated, enthusiastic cadre of international alumni ambassadors around the world can be a valuable resource for institutions and international alumni relations efforts, but establishing an international alumni ambassador program and maintaining affiliated groups requires initial investments, including ambassador training and means of recognizing participants, as well as the knowledge to sustain the program and ongoing modes of assessment. These attributes of successful international alumni ambassador programs are discussed in the following sections.

Train

Offering training sessions and written guidelines that clearly define the responsibilities and boundaries of the international alumni ambassador role creates transparency and common understanding. An online international alumni ambassador handbook or manual overviewing policies and procedures, programming, and training resources may be appropriate with programs requesting (or requiring) more formal approaches, such as those that focus on international marketing and student recruitment.

Handbooks should help international alumni ambassadors learn current information about the university so that they are equipped to both share their personal experiences and educate prospective students about the university. The training manual may start with a welcome letter from university officials, followed by information on the following topics:
- **International alumni ambassador opportunities:** information about each ambassador opportunity, including the purpose of the role, duties, responsibilities of the university, and ambassador dos and don'ts
- **Frequently asked questions:** answers to questions other ambassadors have had about their duties
- **University directory:** phone numbers, email addresses, and websites for student support staff and resources

- **College planning timeline:** steps and tips for prospective students before and during the application process and the timeline for completing each task
- **Key data points and core messaging:** facts and figures, student profiles, list of majors, benefits of attending the university, tuition and fees information, financial aid basics, admissions policies, and brand messaging

Involve current alumni leadership in all facets of the international alumni ambassador training, including planning, facilitating, evaluating, and creating and publishing materials. Embracing the notion of training the trainers secures a better chance that the initial investments in international alumni ambassador training are sustained and strengthened (Dobson 2014).

Recognize

As mentioned in chapter 3, the "R" in the LEARN Model of International Alumni Relations stands for "recognition," which is just as important for supporting and retaining international alumni ambassadors as it is for alumni at large. Developing an annual award for international ambassador volunteerism can be a way to include international alumni ambassadors on awards committees. An awards ceremony may become a centerpiece of a regional event and can involve leadership at all levels in bestowing the award to create a sense of value, respect, and gratitude for recipients' commitment to the university's global vision.

Sustain

Alumni are motivated to engage where there is an opportunity—when they can make a difference and the institution presents activities suiting their values and capabilities. Cultural norms vary, and the ways international alumni ambassadors invest in their relationships with their alma mater may require careful management. Institutions can sustain international alumni ambassador programs and minimize conflicts by keeping in mind the following three tips:

1. Understand the culture of countries of interest (e.g., Does new interest from an alum or family stem from true philanthropy, or is it motivated by a business deal?)
2. Seek advice from trusted international liaisons before deciding to make major investments in international alumni ambassador programs in new or existing markets. Host key contacts on campus or meet in mutually convenient locations to ask for local introductions, gain a sense of how

business is conducted in the country, and receive tips for culturally sensitive business etiquette.
3. Invest early in international alumni ambassador training. Create easy ways for international graduates to become involved early in their alumni life cycle as recruitment partners, and create programs to leverage alumni volunteers as international ambassadors, locally informed fundraising agents, and advocates and allies for the institution.

Assess

Knowing how international alumni ambassadors perceive the benefits of their involvement helps alumni relations officers align opportunities to participants' needs and wants. Surveying international alumni ambassadors on an annual basis will create a useful set of data. The survey can be segmented by region, school, age range, or affinity group (in the case of efforts to organize professional networks). Furthermore, the survey can inform the goals for the coming years. Develop incentives for alumni ambassadors to participate in the survey, such as a random drawing for a bookstore gift card or a box of deluxe university-branded business cards. Most important, set a deadline for replying and then, in turn, produce an executive summary of the feedback to share with all alumni ambassadors worldwide (e.g., "Our global community outside the United States has told us..."). As an added bonus, surveys can drive more alumni to the institution's website to update contact information, search the directory for alumni connections, and find links to the institution's other globally minded pages (e.g., international student services or education abroad).

Developing Performance Measures of International Alumni Ambassador Programs

Institutions that sponsor international alumni ambassador programs will want to ensure the sustainability of these programs through ongoing resource development and support. By providing easily assessable and digestible quantitative and qualitative evidence of the impact of international alumni ambassador programs, alumni relations officers remain proactive and knowledgeable about the influence of their alumni ambassadors and other key stakeholders.

Alumni programs have the strongest impact when the correct set of performance measures and assessment practices is put into place. The use of international alumni

Chapter 4

ambassadors is no different. Former international advancement professional and practicing consultant Mark C. Sollis outlines key steps and considerations in developing performance measures of international alumni ambassador programs.

CASE STUDY

Metrics and the Impact of International Alumni Ambassadors
By Mark C. Sollis

Business Name	D3 Advancement Studio
Motto	To dream, to dare, to do
Primary Services	Strategy, planning, performance management, and coaching
Founded	2018
Locations	Global (registered in Canada)
Website	www.d3advancement.com

Understanding exactly what international alumni ambassadors are attempting to achieve is the critical first step to effectively measuring programs. It is common to see all sorts of metrics used in alumni operations, numbers pulled and some data points reviewed. But significant questions often remain: Why those measures, and what would one actually do with the information to shift strategic focus, make resource decisions, or reset business processes?

Selecting Strong Metrics

For an international alumni ambassador program—or any other international program—having clear, specific objectives (examples included later) can support program growth and effectiveness, lead to a better internal understanding of program impact, and even underpin a case for additional partnerships or resource support. If, for example, the goal of a program is simply to engage more alumni to promote the university, the metrics put in place may measure very little and have even less long-term impact. Perhaps worse, they could lead to the perception of success (e.g., "we have reached more alumni") but leave the newly engaged audience without a clear sense of purpose and the program without the ability to test effectiveness beyond simply building a pool of willing alumni. This may further put the university at risk if the alumni pool is not engaged, tainting alumni's perceptions and influencing their willingness to engage in the future.

Certainly, base measures should include a goal for alumni engagement, including targets for identified market segments (based on affinity levels, demographic profiles, location, etc.). Encourage specific targets, such as first-generation college graduates in a particular Latin American country, rather than one catch-all, such as all international alumni from Latin America.

Metrics should be designed with the strategic focus of the international alumni ambassador program in mind. If the focus is on supporting international student recruitment, set targets related to the success rate of prospective students who engaged with individual international alumni ambassadors. Or, if international alumni ambassadors are asked to convene or lead an alumni community, measure not only the number of alumni engaged, but the awareness within the community of its purpose, how it connects to the university, and the satisfaction of its members. Similarly, study what is not happening. Does the community of 50 engaged international alumni ambassadors look "good on the board" but miss out on a market potential of a few hundred ambassadors? For each area of focus (career support, philanthropic efforts, research, industry connections, etc.), identifying specific targets and discussing them up front should be part of the program development.

Tracking Understanding, Retention, and Satisfaction

Since critical roles for international alumni ambassadors involve acting on institutional priorities, regular assessment of their understanding of these priorities, institutional initiatives, and the goals of the university is also essential. Program directors may assume alumni are well informed because of previous discussions; however, knowledge gaps or lack of clarity can still be present. Test awareness, whether through ongoing and regular monitoring, sampling studies, interviews, or similar methods. Do ambassadors know and accept the institution's recruitment priorities for learners? Do they know which research initiatives would be of specific interest to the institution within a certain market?

Ensure that retention rates of engaged alumni are closely tracked by monitoring the levels of individual alumni's engagement and their experiences through a structured volunteer assessment on a quarterly or semiannual basis. Specifically, look for trends of increasing or decreasing involvement or satisfaction. Rather than focus on a total number, international alumni ambassador programs should pay more attention to ensuring alumni stay engaged, which in the retail world is equivalent to a company retaining their existing customer base as opposed to only chasing new clients.

Lastly, measure satisfaction of the international alumni ambassadors. While it is undoubtedly helpful (and necessary) to spend time with them in conversation to check in, effective assessment goes further than this. Structure interviews with a common set of questions. Conduct focus groups of alumni leaders when challenges or potential opportunities emerge. By collecting both qualitative and quantitative data, institutions will be able to gather a more complete and accurate picture of the experiences of the international alumni ambassadors who engage with the university. As larger trends of engagement and satisfaction become easier to observe and course correct, qualitative assessment will likely provide clarity on some of the challenges and opportunities.

In short:
- Move past volume and feel-good discussions as base indicators of assessment to targeted, deliberate measurement against well-articulated and understood strategic priorities.
- Set and discuss targets, including quantitative measures.
- Build qualitative assessment into practice.
- Be consistent, clear, realistic, and unapologetic in setting and working toward goals with international alumni ambassadors.

Parents and Families as Ambassadors

As previously discussed, a university's population of ambassadors—individuals who the institution can consistently engage to promote its brand and influence its internationalization efforts—extends beyond alumni to other internal and external stakeholders. In fact, some groups who have proved themselves to be top ambassadors for an institution are not alumni, but their relatives. The rest of this chapter focuses on this special population of ambassadors: parents and family members.

Institutions can leverage international parents and families as international ambassadors no matter where they live in the world. Parents and families can offer the same meaningful impact and philanthropic support as do alumni. Having a proven track record of successful and meaningful engagement with a particular international community can lead to in-kind support from international alumni, families, and friends. For example, international parents may offer to host a major reception, such as a capital campaign launch, at their home or club. Parents may also volunteer to serve on an international careers panel or agree to participate in a virtual student recruitment program to talk about their experiences as involved members of the institution's international community. Generous offers from international alumni ambassadors should always be vetted to eliminate any conflict of interest. Reputation and relationships are mutually reinforcing. Careful attention to the relationships between international ambassadors and an institution will safeguard both.

Engaging parents and families is emerging as a priority across many alumni relations offices. The University of Rochester is a model example of a research university that has developed strong relationships with their international parent ambassadors.

CASE STUDY

International Parents as Ambassadors: University of Rochester China Parent Network
By Alyssa Shoup, EdD

Institution	University of Rochester
Motto	*Meliora* (Ever better)
Founded	1850
Location	Rochester, New York
Number of Students	11,744 (33% of which are international)
Number of Alumni	115,000 (10% of which are internationally based)
Department Responsible for International Alumni Relations	Alumni Relations and Advancement
Alumni Relations Office Website	www.rochester.edu/alumni

Relationship Building and the Formation of the China Parent Network

The University of Rochester formally established the China Parent Network in October 2019. Parents in China had been phenomenal informal ambassadors of the university for years, hosting events to build community and promoting the university broadly among their personal networks—all with little support

Chapter 4

from the university. Alumni Relations and Advancement simply did not have relationships with these parents.

With the creation of a dedicated international engagement officer position, the relationship between these parents and the university flourished. The international engagement officer prioritized meeting with them to learn about their activities, goals, and motivations for this volunteer work on behalf of the university. At the fifth annual China Parent Retreat, hosted in Beijing in 2019, the parent leaders stood before an audience of more than 200 fellow parents, eight university staff, and a member of the university's Board of Trustees, pledging to serve as leaders of the University of Rochester China Parent Network.

The China Parent Network Committee (CPNC), a collaborative effort between the parent leaders and the university, was established to formalize this relationship. The CPNC leads the China Parent Network and is responsible for increasing engagement and communication with and among Rochester parents to advocate for and support students and alumni. They are instrumental in facilitating communication between the University of Rochester and fellow parents across China, mobilizing around key goals and priorities, and responding quickly to the needs of fellow parents, the students, and the institution. The CPNC works closely with Alumni Relations and Advancement and is the communication conduit between the greater parent population across China and campus partners who aid in information flow and mobilization around key initiatives. Figure 1 depicts the stakeholders who constitute campus partners, Alumni Relations and Advancement, the CPNC, and the China Parent Network.

Figure 1. China Parent Network Stakeholders

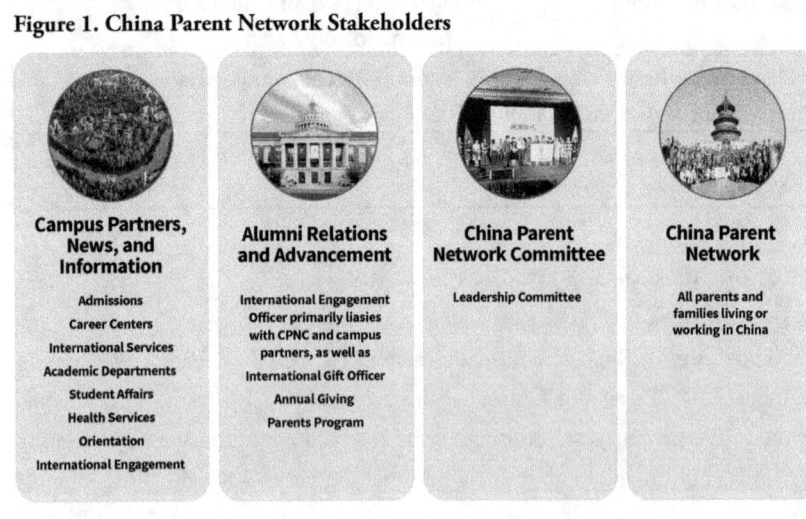

Goals and Activities of the China Parent Network

The goals of the China Parent Network are jointly created with the university and CPNC and include
1. strengthening the relationship and communication between parents and families of Chinese students at the University of Rochester;
2. supporting the academic and cocurricular experience of Chinese and other international students;
3. supporting the career development of all international students and alumni; and
4. promoting the University of Rochester in China.

Model Practices and Advice

From this successful partnership with international parent ambassadors, the following practices and advice have emerged:
1. Communicate to internal stakeholders the goals, objectives, and value proposition for supporting international parent and family engagement.
2. Dedicate staff to international alumni and parent engagement.
3. Build on and strengthen key campus partnerships and identify how parents can participate in and advocate for particular areas (e.g., recruitment and career placement).
4. Articulate goals and objectives with parent leaders, and collaboratively create a structure for and calendar of communications, meetings, and activities that best match the interests of parents, families, students, and the institution.
5. Start small and build for sustainability.
6. Ensure international parent leaders are included in larger volunteer training, recognition, and stewardship programs that the institution has in place.

Conclusion

International alumni ambassador programs require investments to ensure the ambassador experience is thoughtful, satisfying, respectful, beneficial, and personal. The impact is felt as increasing numbers of international alumni ambassadors systematically promote their alma mater's brand abroad, so that others can join their community and benefit as those who came before. Today's growing interest across the world in developing relationships with international alumni and stakeholders, such as parents and families, widens the circle of participation between constituents. Many more players emerge as new agenda items begin to focus on the influence of international alumni ambassadors to serve both short- and long-term internationalization goals.

References and Additional Resources

Dobson, Gretchen. 2014. *International Travel Handbook: Engaging Constituents Abroad.* Denver, CO: Academic Impressions.

Dobson, Gretchen. 2016. "Global Alumni Relations Course." *Academic Assembly.* https://aai.onlinetrainingnow.com/courses/global-alumni-relations-course.

Dobson, Gretchen. 2020. "Why It's a Good Idea to Build Academic Alumni Communities." *Times Higher Education.* October 9. https://www.timeshighereducation.com/career/why-its-good-idea-build-academic-alumni-communities.

Unangst, Lisa. 2020. "International Alumni Engagement: Operations, Leadership, and Policy at U.S. Research Universities." *Journal of Higher Education Policy and Leadership Studies* 1, 2:63–77.

University of Minnesota. n.d. *Alumni Ambassador Handbook: A Guide to the University of Minnesota Twin Cities.* https://admissions.tc.umn.edu/PDFs/alumni_ambassador.pdf.

Chapter 5
Transformational Philanthropy: Alumni Giving to Advance the International Agenda

By Maria Gallo, EdD, and Kevin Fleming, PhD

The international alumni spirit of giving received media attention when the COVID-19 pandemic threw the world into lockdown in early 2020. Alumni across the globe mobilized to help international students stranded in their country of study by donating to special bursaries and relief funds. International alumni in China, for instance, contacted the International Office at University College Cork (UCC) to ask what they could do to support their alma mater (Echo Live 2020). As a result, the group coordinated fundraising efforts among fellow alumni in China to purchase personal protective equipment for frontline health care workers linked to the Irish university. From crisis, an international community emerged, leading to the establishment of the UCC alumni chapters in Beijing and Shanghai as a long-term way to stay connected and respond to future philanthropic support efforts.

The feat of the UCC alumni in China is hardly an isolated incident, as international alumni have a long history of philanthropic allyship with their alma maters. This chapter focuses on the generosity of alumni giving through philanthropy, traditionally defined as financial donations that contribute to the international agenda of the institution. Alumni and philanthropy are often viewed as synonymous, and building relationships with alumni is recognized as a means toward a philanthropic end—asking and receiving donations from alumni. However, as the premise of this book demonstrates, alumni generosity is broad in scope. Alumni can be involved in philanthropic giving by volunteering their time and talent, and these nonmonetary contributions can have as much, or even more, of a profound impact on the internationalization imprint. International alumni can play myriad important roles related to philanthropy: serving as a member of a regional or national alumni chapter; identifying and, as appropriate, qualifying prospective donors; acting as cultural attachés, guides, or hosts for their university's local visits; providing diplomatic assistance when institutions navigate local regulatory matters; offering pro bono banking and legal advice; and serving on committees or councils for fundraising campaigns.

Transformational Philanthropy

Despite this broadened definition of philanthropy as time, talent, and treasure, this chapter focuses on fundraising, with an emphasis on transformational philanthropy. In her book on transformational philanthropy, Lisa M. Dietlin (2010, xiv) outlines a definition for this concept that can be adapted for an international alumni context: "By *transformational*, I mean a philanthropic donation that changes the course of or has a tremendous impact on a nonprofit organization." While Dietlin focuses on the potential of transformational philanthropy within nonprofits and entrepreneurial spheres, this chapter considers how philanthropy involving alumni is transformational to advancing the international agendas of higher education institutions. Therefore, transformational philanthropy with an international alumni lens considers how donors select, invest, and value the transformational impact of internationalization for students or for the institution.

From an operational perspective, international philanthropy is often characterized as attracting donations from international sources, such as alumni living abroad. Complexities and differences around philanthropy persist across political, historical, geographic, and cultural dimensions as well as religious traditions, which can influence the approach to international fundraising appeals (Moody and Breeze 2016). While this goes beyond the scope of the chapter, Michael Moody and Beth Breeze's book *The Philanthropy Reader* (2016) illuminates many of the debates that might be useful in fully understanding the particular contexts that influence the ways in which philanthropy can operate at an institution and their impact on fundraising within international realms. Adames (2019) is another great resource to provide additional understanding of the mechanics of fundraising from international sources.

This chapter instead focuses on the intersection between philanthropy, alumni, and internationalization and the powerful potential for alumni donations to enhance internationalization or support international efforts. As with many fundraising efforts, reaching out to a specific group of prospective donors who have had a shared experience is more likely to lead to success. International alumni may be more enthusiastic about giving to a bursary fund to support future international students from their home country. More broadly, international alumni may also value supporting internationalization efforts across campus. These are only small components of such connections between philanthropy, alumni, and internationalization, and this chapter presents a broader perspective on these connections.

At this point, it should be noted that this chapter presents the advancement of the international agenda within an institution as transformational. Internationalization leads to valuable student experiences, growth, and perspectives. Students build global competence while the campus community gains diversity, understanding, and collaboration. Therefore, institutions are increasingly prioritizing philanthropy that funds internationalization efforts.

This chapter offers an original framework to build transformational philanthropy within an institution and enhance the intersection between philanthropy, alumni, and internationalization. There are three strategic elements that need to be aligned for transformational philanthropy to advance the international agenda:

1. **The anchor:** alignment across the overall institutional mission, values, vision, and strategy
2. **The lens:** priorities identified within the institution's international strategy
3. **The landscape:** institutional context that encompasses key constituents, including alumni, as well as on-campus and external stakeholders

Figure 1 shows how the alignment between these three elements creates the potential for transformational philanthropy to advance the international agenda.

Figure 1. Framework for Transformational Philanthropy to Advance the Internationalization Agenda

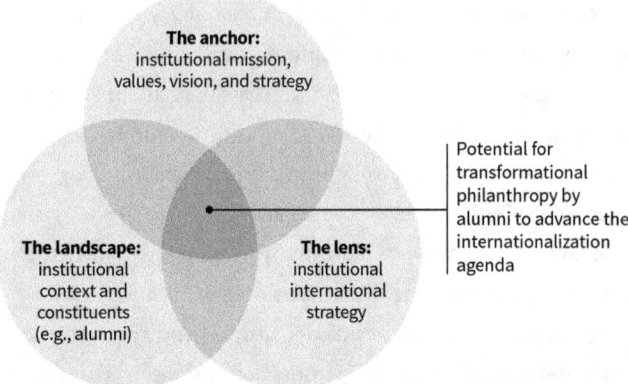

The overlap between these three strategic elements within an institution enables transformational philanthropy. In this chapter, these elements are explored, offering examples of how the resulting synergies contribute to engaging alumni in philanthropic efforts to impact internationalization.

Increasingly, higher education institutions develop, launch, and promote strategic plans and mission statements that anchor their values and vision for the future. Institutional mission, values, vision, and strategy (noted as "the anchor" in figure 1) offer context for institutions' international strategies. An increased emphasis on internationalization within institutions is accompanied by an internal infrastructure—international office and internationalization strategy (noted as "the lens" in figure 1). Finally, "the landscape" refers to the institutional context, from internal and external stakeholders—including alumni—along with the climate in which an institution operates, influencing its potential for transformational philanthropy.

The Anchor: Institutional Mission, Vision, Values, and Strategy

Adames (2019) emphasizes the importance of integrating international philanthropy within the wider institution: "A robust international advancement strategy should not be a separate entity but rather part of the overall strategy for a college or university—linked to enrollment, corporate relations, and parent and alumni programs, as well as the development operation." These conditions are even more important if transformational philanthropy goals relate to internationalization, articulate a case for support, and are actively pursued by the institution's development (fundraising) team.

In order for internationalization to be truly transformational for the institution and students, it must first be embraced and embodied within the values, mission, and vision of the institution. Mission and vision statements are often included in institutional strategic plans and increasingly describe global-facing and international imprints as part of the values, likely including words such as "inclusion" and "diversity," which can resonate with an internationalization agenda. Common phrases such as "creating social change" and "public engagement" also invite the potential for internationalization to manifest at an institutional level.

To translate these broad, institutional statements into a strategic argument for advancing the international agenda, it is necessary to write a case for support. These case statements are a "logical compelling rationale…[that] should be concise, accurate, on target and above all easily read" (Tromble 1998). How often do international marketing materials offer a concise, accurate, and compelling rationale to attract international students? Similarly, a case for philanthropic support focuses these same energies to ensure a compelling narrative can be made to alumni, illustrating the transformational impact of internationalization and enticing them to invest financially toward furthering these values at their alma mater.

As a strong example of a philanthropic anchor, the Office of Advancement at Queen's University in Ontario, Canada, makes an impassioned argument for internationalization to donors, anchored to the institution's strategic priorities, mission, and values. First, Queen's Advancement Strategic Priorities include a focus on "Sustainable Engagement with International Alumni," anchoring the institution's international context and aspirations. Next, the anchor integrates with the university's international plan (the lens), outlining priorities including "International Research Engagement," "International Mobility," "International Enrollment Management," and "International at Home," articulating the institution's commitment to "international prominence" and "internationalization principles" (Queen's University 2015). The plan emphasizes that the community, including alumni, shares the responsibility to build internationalization at the institution, aligning funding priorities to the transformative impact that advancing the international agenda at the institution can have on the student experience, international research, and for the overall campus community.

The Lens: The International Plan

Increasingly, colleges and universities see the value of having a concerted international plan that encourages international growth in academics, research, and strategic initiatives at the institution—constituting the lens. Like other strategic planning documents, an international plan is ambitious, outlining a clear direction to advance the international agenda. The emphasis on international university rankings, and more recent iterations such as sustainability rankings, positions higher education institutions within a wider international ecosystem, vying not only for increased ranking position but also documenting how the work of the institution contributes to enhancing local, regional, and even the international communities.

More than 2 decades ago, Jane Knight (1994) presented an internationalization cycle. She argued that the awareness of and commitment to international work by key stakeholders within an institution leads to the thoughtful planning and subsequent operational mechanics required for internationalization work to be realized. This incremental approach presents great avenues for engaging international alumni in philanthropy. At multiple stages of Knight's internationalization framework, opportunities arise to consider how additional resources—including philanthropic funding—can work toward advancing the international agenda.

International alumni should be explicitly noted as strategic partners within any international plan, as they have a great deal to contribute to the international agenda. In addition, international alumni can become key actors to facilitate philanthropic giving or provide financial donations to develop an institution's internationalization ambitions—especially if the initiatives offer transformative experiences for students or even fellow alumni. In her research, Lisa Childress (2009, 291) presents a definition of internationalization plans that aligns with the engagement of key stakeholders: "Such plans advance institutional goals for internationalization by expressing institutional commitment, defining institutional goals, informing stakeholders' participation, as well as informing and stimulating stakeholder involvement in internationalization initiatives."

While it is not unusual to see testimonials from international students or alumni in marketing materials for student recruitment purposes, an equal opportunity exists for stories of international alumni to help build a lens for transformational internationalization. Internationalization offers growth for individual students or alumni, while also striving toward the aforementioned institutional priorities. In this context, philanthropy can be positioned as a way to advance transformative internationalization aspirations.

Mary Cronin (2020), president of the Wishing Chair Foundation, an organization that funds educational travel to Ireland, outlined the transformative impact of her study abroad experience as a teenager in the 1990s: "These influential experiences mapped the course of my career." As a member of the Irish diaspora in the United States, going to Ireland for a few weeks initially seemed like a nice way to connect with her ancestry. She participated in the inaugural study abroad group organized by the Institute of Study Abroad Ireland (ISAI). Two decades later, ISAI focuses on faculty-led study abroad programs: "Our mission remains simple—to help students become more culturally competent and internationalized by using…all aspects of Ireland as a platform for developing comparative and critical thinking" (ISAI 2020). In 2019, ISAI launched the Wishing Chair Foundation, with alum Cronin as executive director. The purpose of the foundation is to reinforce the mission of the ISAI to make study abroad available to everyone.

Philanthropic efforts for the program through the Wishing Chair Foundation focus on providing short-term study abroad programs for underrepresented students in study abroad. For instance, Niamh Hamill, PhD, founder and academic director of ISAI, explains how the history of Ireland has resonated with Black students: "African American students discovered that the civil rights movement in Ireland in 1968 was modeled on the American civil rights movement…and the shared narrative of discrimination, segregation, and persecution." This is just one example of how the values of a diversity-centered internationalization program serve as anchors; alumni who have had this transformational internationalization experience are the landscape for the Foundation, offering the lens, or impetus, for giving philanthropically.

The foundation's prospectus provides a compelling case for support for donors:

> We believe that all students should be given opportunities to explore and learn about the world, regardless of their background or financial situation. And research supports our thesis that study abroad changes lives. (Wishing Chair Foundation 2020)

The future of the foundation is to support the mobilization of past ISAI study abroad participants, establishing regional chapters so that funds raised in one region benefit students from that region. The foundation is a means for alumni to give someone else a transformative study abroad experience similar to their own or to organize fundraising initiatives with fellow alumni and faculty. Philanthropic giving from alumni enables students and graduates with a shared experience of study abroad to maintain and foster the lens of internationalization they received through an international experience.

Chapter 5

The Landscape: The Operational Environment

The landscape refers to the circumstances within which the institution operates—the cultural contexts, customs, norms, and values in which alumni reside, as well as the culture of internationalization in the campus community. It encompasses the alumni, students, and parents who are either from other countries, currently reside in other countries, or have international experiences as students or at some point during their lives. Landscape also refers to the resource allocations of budget, staffing, and time that are critical to enacting espoused internationalization values, priorities, and strategies.

The internationalization landscape of an institution works in concert with its anchor and lens. As the institution increasingly prioritizes internationalization and looks for avenues to incorporate it into its international plans, these values must be matched with accompanying funds, people, and time. Otherwise, they will be no more than value holograms with little substance behind them.

The institutional community must be given time to understand what an internationalization focus means for the institution and its respective departments and to develop contextually savvy strategies that grow the internationalization agenda. The institutional lens that is developed—the strategy for achieving internationalization goals—must be informed by an accurate assessment of the current state of internationalization at the institution; its strengths, weaknesses, and areas for growth; and realistic benchmarks that account for allocated resources and institutional context.

For philanthropic purposes, this means that time is given to advancement professionals to (1) situate their understanding of the current state of fundraising with an international perspective, (2) identify opportunities for growth, (3) develop realistic fundraising goals, and (4) optimally employ resources in a way that is appropriate to realizing institutional aspirations. As the institution's internationalization anchor (values, vision, and priorities) are developed, the institutional landscape (the set of circumstances it finds itself within) and lens (internationalization strategy) inform one another. The internationalization aspirations of an institution create a framework for the strategies it uses to achieve its goals, which are informed by the available resources. Reciprocally, prioritizing internationalization can lead to increased resources that alter the institutional landscape and allow for more robust strategies to achieve internationalization goals.

An example of the landscape of transformational philanthropy can be seen at Wageningen University & Research (WUR) in the Netherlands. At regular intervals, alumni stakeholders receive an invitation from the university to participate in revising the strategic plan and to join in the dialogue (Wageningen University & Research 2019). The University Fund Wageningen aligns its goals with the strategic plan, focusing on the role that alumni giving to the fund will have on the global imprint of WUR. It is this integration of the mission of the university, the international dimension, and the operational landscape (the dedicated time, people, and process) that leads alumni to have a transformational effect on the university strategy and on wider society.

> To situate an institution's anchor, lens, and landscape, there are certain questions advancement professionals can ask:
> - **To what degree does the campus community have an international presence?**
>   - Are there significant numbers of international students who attend the institution, and where are they from?
>   - Do a significant number of students study abroad (currently and historically)?
>   - How broadly distributed are the countries to which students travel through study abroad programs?
> - **To what degree does the institutional anchor (the mission, vision, values, and strategy) create an environment that emphasizes internationalization and facilitate conditions through which to pursue an international fundraising agenda?**
>   - To what degree are colleagues across campus savvy in their awareness of, approach to, and navigation within internationalization spaces?
> - **How does the institutional landscape inform the internationalization lens?**
>   - Are international values and priorities supported with budgetary and staffing allocations that allow the institution to pursue its institutional fundraising strategies?
>   - How do resources shape the internationalization fundraising strategies, and how can these resources be optimally dedicated to internationalization fundraising initiatives?
>   - Where do the intersections of international alumni and parent populations in different countries, along with staffing and budget resources, suggest that the institution concentrate its fundraising efforts?

Putting It All Together: Tecnológico de Monterrey

Tecnológico de Monterrey, a private university in Mexico, provides a useful example of how the anchor, lens, and landscape intertwine through alumni philanthropy.

Transformation is woven throughout the strategic plan at Tecnológico de Monterrey (the anchor). These threads of transformation are part of the institution's ambitions for its students, referred to as Tec21. Tec21 includes the skills and competencies students need to be leaders in the twenty-first century, including critical thinking, ethics, citizenship and social responsibility, proficiency in foreign languages, and global perspective (Tecnológico de Monterrey 2020). The Leaders of Tomorrow (Líderes del Mañana) project is a Tec21 initiative (the lens) with a succinct mission: "Ensure that young Mexicans with high leadership potential but with limited financial resources can have access to, and be able to study and grow at, the Tecnológico de Monterrey" (Tecnológico de Monterrey 2020, 26). This initiative has translated into a clear case for support for scholarships for Mexican students to participate in a higher education experience committed to achieving these global competencies (Tecnológico de Monterrey 2017).

Alumni have contributed through events such as reunions, where funds are raised to directly support the Leaders of Tomorrow scholarships, with other regional events building on local stories of the project's impact in southern and western Mexico (the landscape). The stories of the Leaders of Tomorrow student participants have also resonated with international alumni.

This case depicts the alignment of all three components of the transformational philanthropy framework—the anchor, lens, and landscape—through an example of how even micro levels of internationalization with individual students can motivate alumni to donate and create positive stories of student success. Even if the efforts are small, the transformational impact on the individual remains significant. In celebrating small transformational experiences as a result of philanthropy, there is potential to create momentum for broader, deeper levels of transformational experiences, in this case for students across the entire Leaders of Tomorrow project and beyond.

Involving International Alumni in Transformational Philanthropy

How do institutions bring alumni and the international agenda together for transformational philanthropy? The previous sections show how the anchor, the lens, and the landscape collectively spur transformational philanthropy. Figure 2 extends this concept to show how transformational philanthropy happens within practical operations at an institution. Additional considerations arise surrounding how to directly involve alumni in the practical work that gives rise to transformational philanthropy.

Figure 2. Transformational Philanthropy Within the Institution

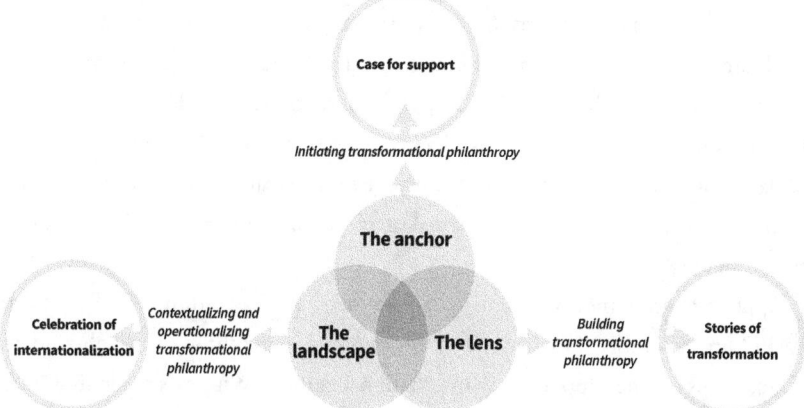

As previously expressed, transformational philanthropy is defined as giving that has an impact on the international agenda and mobilizes internationalization. Within each of the components of the internationalization framework (anchor, lens, and landscape), actions can be taken to facilitate transformational philanthropy. Rather than passive observers, alumni play active roles in shaping and pursuing internationalization aspirations.

First, the mission, vision, values, and strategy of the institution (the anchor) lay the groundwork for transformational philanthropy, underpinned by a persuasive case for support. International alumni should be active players in devising the case for support to ensure it resonates with other alumni who will become ambassadors and donors. The case for support to advance the international agenda is only strengthened with direct stakeholder involvement.

Next, the international plan serves as a lens to build transformational philanthropy. International alumni stories can personify the transformative impact of internationalization efforts that are part of the international plan, growing a case for support. International educators and advancement professionals can work together to identify and promote these alumni stories, reinforcing the impact of both internationalization and (eventually) the philanthropic giving to these efforts. The authenticity of these stories has the potential to initiate and build a culture of philanthropic giving in international circles. These alumni can then be identified, recognized, and promoted by their alma mater as an important piece in the transformational philanthropy puzzle.

Finally, the context and the constituents involved play a crucial role in transformational philanthropy. Special events in person or even online are ways to celebrate internationalization and create the conditions for alumni to participate in philanthropic giving that impacts the international agenda. As was shown in the examples throughout this chapter, this framework for transformational philanthropy also has spinoff effects, especially in creating international alumni communities that are active in personal or professional pursuits and give back to their alma mater.

Applying the framework depicted in figure 2, the case study of Universidad EAFIT in Colombia shows how transformational philanthropy through student scholarships can be supported by international alumni. With this student-alumni continuum, EAFIT aims to raise awareness across the community of the impact of philanthropy to foster potential international alumni support for the future.

CASE STUDY

Alumni as Leaders in (and Recipients of) Transformational Philanthropy: Universidad EAFIT

By Maria Gallo, EdD, with Isabel Cristina Gómez Yepes, MBA

Institution	Universidad EAFIT
Motto	*Inspira Crea Transforma* (Inspire, Create, Transform)
Founded	1960
Location	Medellín, Colombia
Number of Students in 2020	12,000 (2% of which are international)
Number of Alumni in 2020	55,000

Departments Responsible for International Alumni Relations	• Dirección de Desarrollo Institucional y Egresados (Institutional Development and Alumni Direction) • Centro de Egresados (Alumni Center) • Centro de Filantropía (Philanthropy Center) • Oficina de Relaciones Internacionales (International EAFIT)
Relevant Offices' Websites	• Alumni Center: https://www.eafit.edu.co/egresados/Paginas/canal-de-egresados.aspx • Philanthropy Center: https://www.eafit.edu.co/institucional/centro-filantropia/Paginas/inicio.aspx • ORI EAFIT: https://www.eafit.edu.co/international/esp/ori-eafit/Paginas/ori-eafit.aspx

"Inspire, Create, Transform" is the motto of Universidad EAFIT in Medellín, Colombia. A comprehensive university with three branch campuses and about 12,000 students, EAFIT embodies its motto, values, and vision through its emphasis on strategies related to sustainability and an ambition for creating a national and international imprint in the local community.

Recently, EAFIT restructured its organization to include a new advancement office: Institutional Development and Alumni Relations Direction. This office leads both the Alumni and Philanthropy Centers and strengthens their relationships with alumni as it seeks new ambassadors for the institution as well as new donors.

Twenty percent of the students at EAFIT benefit from scholarships as they progress into higher education. The scholarship funding comes from the wider community, including international alumni who make donations to the effort.

EAFIT's website puts donations front and center with a "donate here" button on the university's homepage; however, the importance of these scholarships goes beyond short-term marketing. For more than 15 years, these scholarships have supported hundreds of students. As part of the stewardship efforts, EAFIT has featured in their communication efforts the far-reaching impact of alumni who secured these philanthropy-supported scholarships in the past. These stories of the achievements of past scholarship recipients reinforce the case for the ongoing need for these scholarships and the transformation they have on the lives of students who would not otherwise be able to access higher education.

Many alumni have contributed to the Philanthropy Center of EAFIT since its creation. That is the case of Mónica Hernández, an alum of the systems engineering program who benefited from an EAFIT scholarship fund years ago. Now, having a successful career in the United States as the CEO and founder of MAS Global Consulting, Hernández decided to create her own scholarship program for women in engineering.

EAFIT also launched a campaign for student support. Worried about how the COVID-19 pandemic would result in even more financial burdens on students, including international students, the university initiated a fundraising campaign for a special bursary program, Solidarity Starts at Home. Resonating with the EAFIT alumni community in Colombia, the campaign served 200 students in the first 3 months and benefited from donations from 970 donors, including alumni worldwide.

The international impact of EAFIT's Philanthropy Center can be seen both by the international alumni who contributed to or benefited from philanthropic financial support, along with the broadened internationalization experiences of students who continue to receive the support throughout their studies. EAFIT aligns clearly with the transformational philanthropy framework presented here, devising a compelling case for support, promoting stories of transformation related to internationalization, and creating platforms on campus and online to celebrate internationalization emanating from philanthropic efforts.

Events Centered on Philanthropy

Creating a collaborative landscape so that institutions are open to philanthropic giving for internationalization priorities requires the willingness and involvement of other professionals, including international alumni, to be directly involved in philanthropic giving efforts (see West 2018). The University of Michigan's Pan-Asia Alumni Reunion is a case in point. There is widespread ownership over this flagship event; units across the university and international alumni are directly involved in planning and setting the event's strategic philanthropy aims.

CASE STUDY

Flagship Giving: Pan-Asia Alumni Reunion at the University of Michigan
By Eun Ja Yu

Institution	University of Michigan
Motto	*Artes, scientia, veritas* (Arts, knowledge, truth)
Founded	1817
Location	Ann Arbor, Michigan
Number of Students	31,000 undergraduates on the Ann Arbor campus (14% of which are international)
Number of Alumni	More than 600,000
Department Responsible for International Alumni Relations	Alumni Association of the University of Michigan (AAUM)
Alumni Relations Office Website	https://alumni.umich.edu/

The University of Michigan (U-M) has more than 100 top-ranked programs and is one of the leading research universities in the world (U-M 2020). The Alumni Association of the University of Michigan (AAUM) is an independent, worldwide organization that has more than 600,000 alumni in 179 countries. For more than 125 years, AAUM has been connecting alumni across the globe to each other and the university. The majority of alumni reside in the United States; however, a growing number of international alumni are settling across the globe and are interested in staying connected after leaving Ann Arbor. AAUM engages international alumni through events such as the Pan-Asia Alumni Reunion, networking receptions, and club events. It has also created opportunities for U-M leaders to connect with alumni where they live. The International Giving and Engagement Team and AAUM work collaboratively with university constituents, including international alumni, students, parents, faculty and staff, global corporations, and governmental entities. They have a mandate to cultivate philanthropic relationships with high-capacity donors, deepen U-M communities around the globe through a variety of events and engagement activities, and raise U-M's visibility among key stakeholders in target markets. These activities require identifying and developing strategic relationships across campus that can help advance U-M's academic and research missions. Such relationships can provide sources of funding, platforms for collaborative research, and partners for student and faculty exchange.

The flagship event, the Pan-Asia Alumni Reunion, is an annual event open to all U-M alumni, family, and friends. It was started 10 years ago by a group of alumni in Singapore who wanted to remain connected to each other. The gathering has now turned into the largest U-M event outside of the United States and celebrates the institution's alumni and donors in the region. This event aligns with the mandate to cultivate relationships with alumni and raise U-M's visibility. The Pan-Asia Alumni Reunion allows alumni to reminisce together about their time at U-M, enjoy a cultural showcase, and hear from inspirational local alumni and U-M speakers. It has attracted volunteers, prospective donors, current donors, and friends of the university. The event has been hosted in Hong Kong, Seoul, Shanghai, Singapore, Taipei, and Tokyo. It is an embedded part of the wider U-M international alumni calendar, promoted through the U-M alumni website and open to all alumni in the region.

The Pan-Asia Alumni Scholarship was established in 2014 by alumni in Hong Kong to honor the reunion. Each year, alumni in Asia and around the world give to the scholarship in celebration of future generations of students. Funds are raised in the form of sponsorships and registration fees that include a scholarship portion. The scholarship provides financial aid in support of outstanding undergraduate students from across Asia attending U-M. To date, AAUM has raised more than $250,000 and awarded six scholarships.

As AAUM continues to grow its activities overseas, strategic guidance and philanthropic support will be key. With this in mind, the CEO recruited an international advisory council. The group includes established and emerging leaders well-positioned to help the organization expand its brand and services around the globe.

Conclusion

Alumni, especially those with international experiences, are pivotal players in initiating, building, and securing transformational internationalization through philanthropic giving. No longer are alumni solely the responsibility of the alumni relations function within the institution; it is essential that international educators and other university administrators see the value of international alumni, including their ability to advance the international agenda through philanthropy. Just as an internationalization agenda detailed within strategic and international plans permeates the entire institution, international educators can also benefit from becoming boundary-spanners who work across the institution to educate colleagues about the benefits of internationalization. As alumni relations professionals, advancement marketers, and fundraisers build international ties, they can connect more powerfully with a base of alumni passionate about internationalization and ensure that internationalization is high on the philanthropy agenda of the institution. These collaborative efforts promise to create the transformational philanthropy that provides seminal, defining experiences for students, alumni, and the wider institutional community.

References

Adames, Ivan A. 2019. "International and Global Fundraising." In *Advancing Higher Education: New Strategies for Fundraising, Philanthropy and Engagement*, eds. Michael J. Worth and Matthew T. Lambert. London: Rowman & Littlefield Publishers.

Childress, Lisa K. 2009. "Internationalization Plans for Higher Education Institutions." *Journal of Studies in International Education* 13, 3:289–309.

Cronin, Mary. 2020. Interview. July 14, 2020.

Dietlin, Lisa M. 2010. *Transformational Philanthropy: Entrepreneurs and Nonprofits*. London: Jones and Bartlett Publishers.

Echo Live. 2020. "UCC Alumni in China Donate Funds Towards PPE for Cork Healthcare Workers." April 24. https://www.echolive.ie/corknews/arid-40127354.html.

Institute of Study Abroad Ireland (ISAI). 2020. "About Us." https://isaireland.com/about-us/.

Knight, Jane. 1994. "Internationalization: Elements and Checkpoints." *Canadian Bureau for International Education Research*, 7:1–15.

Moody, Michael, and Beth Breeze. 2016. *The Philanthropy Reader*. Abingdon, UK: Routledge.

Queen's University, Office of the Association Vice-Principal International. 2015. *Comprehensive International Plan 2015–2019*. Kingston, Ontario: Queen's University. https://www.queensu.ca/sites/default/files/assets/pages/strategicframework/QU-2015-Comp-International-Plan-acc.pdf.

Tecnológico de Monterrey. 2017. "Supporting Talent with Higher Education." Lideres del Mañana and Tecnológico de Monterrey. https://www.case.org/system/files/media/file/BrochureIRR.pdf.

Tecnológico de Monterrey. 2020. *2020 Strategic Plan*. http://sitios.itesm.mx/webtools/planestrategico2020/publico/EN/document/2020StrategicPlan.pdf.

Tromble, William W. 1998. *Excellence in Advancement: Applications for Higher Education and Nonprofit Organizations*. Frederick, MD: Aspen Publishers.

University of Michigan (U-M). 2020. "Facts and Figures." https://umich.edu/facts-figures/.

Wageningen University & Research. 2019. *Strategic Plan Wageningen University & Research 2019-2022*. January 2. https://issuu.com/wageningenur/docs/cc_strategicplan_uk_lr.

West, Charlotte. 2018. "Funding Internationalization Through Creative Collaboration." *International Educator*, November/December. https://www.nafsa.org/ie-magazine/2018/11/1/funding-internationalization-through-creative-collaboration.

Wishing Chair Foundation. 2020. *Wishing Chair Foundation Prospectus 2020: Supporting Educational Experiences in Ireland*. https://static1.squarespace.com/static/5e6ce0208e7ad24f4e0fd188/t/5e6e3cb421ba4c5543319292/1584282811144/WCF+Prospectus+AG+v1.3.pdf.

Chapter 6
The Roles of International Alumni: Perspectives from the Field

As explored throughout the previous chapters, institutions have a wealth of opportunities to engage international alumni both at home and abroad. However, staff who work with international alumni may be used to receiving skeptical questions from leadership: "Why do we need to build and sustain these relationships when international alumni only make up X percent of our entire alumni base? What value do these networks bring to our institution?" These decision-makers may be unfamiliar with the accomplishments of international alumni at other institutions or curious about what comparable programs look like.

Specific motives for investing in international alumni relations programs vary; however, as discussed in chapter 1, common reasons include (1) higher education's service missions; (2) global talent and innovation; (3) economic impact; and (4) global problem-solving. Chapter 6 hones in on related outcomes of real-life international alumni programs, presenting numerous model practice examples of how educational institutions and organizations are activating international alumni to advance internationalization priorities. The sections in chapter 6 take deeper dives into the themes of brand and reputation management, recruitment and retention of talent, employability for the twenty-first century, and innovation and social responsibility.

Brand and Reputation Management

Alignment between an alumni association's brand and an institutional brand can provide support for core values, such as diversity, inclusiveness, learning partnerships, and global citizenship. In this way, international alumni networks and chapters become an extension of the institutional and alumni brand. By "thinking globally, acting locally," international alumni groups communicate these core values through programs designed to fit the local context and engage and support alumni, families, students, and prospective students. Brand affinity toward an institution is reinforced when it is shared through social media, added to a LinkedIn profile, and sought after in job searches.

Recruitment and Retention of Talent

Competition prompts colleges and universities to adopt strategic enrollment management plans that include marketing the institution to international students (Dobson 2015). Institutions can turn to their former international students to help promote the institution abroad. Indeed, the success of an institution's graduates became a cornerstone of many marketing and recruitment campaigns at home and abroad. Locally organized international alumni chapters and families provide in-person testimonials and answer prospective students' questions. Engaged alumni share their educational experience virtually and extend their influence through the use of social media.

Employability for the Twenty-First Century

Technological disruptions in all industries have forced higher education to rethink the competencies and skills needed for students to participate in the current and future labor markets. International alumni can play important roles as conduits between students, the labor market, and global needs. An institution with established international alumni relationships may call on international alumni and international alumni chapters to help the college or university advise students and manage expectations surrounding educational and workplace experiences. They can also advise institutions on curriculum development, mentor students, and offer physical and virtual internships and job placements. Additionally, institutions can take ownership for enhancing employability during alumni's lifetimes by creating clear lines of communication between alumni who seek opportunities to expand their professional knowledge and partnerships through lifelong learning.

Innovation and Social Responsibility

Universities' public and private partnerships are evidenced in their focus on supporting the United Nations's Sustainable Development Goals and maintaining active roles alongside industries as coproducers of innovation and research. Given universities' roles in innovation, international alumni can be strategic partners as entrepreneurs and innovators, advancing research and development around the world. By remaining connected to the alma mater, industry, and government, international alumni forge trusted relationships among all stakeholders. Additionally, international alumni public diplomacy strategies can leverage the potential of alumni networks. It is important to note, however, that public diplomacy is not entirely self-interested. It rests on the mutuality that comes from two-way relationship-building, an overall value proposition that understands, respects, and responds to the interests of international alumni. Institutions supporting international alumni engagement enable these benefits and are, in effect, champions to wider organizational or alumni agendas where the notion of knowledge diplomacy is central.

Reference

Dobson, Gretchen, ed. 2015. *Staying Global: How International Alumni Relations Advances the Agenda*. Amsterdam, The Netherlands: European Association for International Education.

Chapter 6

Brand and Reputation Management

Getting noticed is the first step in marketing international higher education to external stakeholders (Sofiri 2020). Early actions include awareness marketing, whereby brand awareness is built through means such as social media, mobile platforms, and digital advertising.

This section begins with an overview of brand and reputation management and traces the stages of how brands are established, evolved, and leveraged over the life cycles of students and alumni, many of whom wear the moniker of international or global brand ambassador. A marketing expert on international student recruitment with Jackfruit Marketing sets the stage for the examples that follow of how institutions and other international education stakeholders form partnerships that boost visibility for the university in key markets. Examples in this chapter cover branding in graduate programs, from the perspective of Fordham University Law School, and the benefits of involving highly engaged young alumni as members of a global ambassador community, as told by Northeastern University. Impactrics, a New York-based alumni relations company, takes a fresh look at alumni international travel and how sponsored group programs build brand affinity. This is followed by a look at the concept of multiple affinities and how institutions (and alumni) leverage opportunities to build their respective brands with expanded networks. The final section highlights how state or provincial governments, such as those in Australia, are incorporating international alumni ambassadors as key representatives to further the educational brand and opportunities to tap markets overseas.

International Alumni and Brand Development

International higher education is marked by increasing competition among institutions around the world, and one way institutions differentiate themselves from one another is by building brand affinity and community among their stakeholders, beginning with prospective students and families and carried throughout alumni's lives. Fostering brands and managing reputations require ample resources and know-how for the institution to be successful at the onset.

CASE STUDY

How Institutions Can Engage International Alumni to Build Their Brand
By Jacqueline Kassteen

Business Name	Jackfruit Marketing
Motto	Marketing and branding expertise for international student recruitment
Primary Services	Consultancy, project management, and training for professional development in marketing, brand strategy, content, and storytelling
Founded	2016
Locations	United Kingdom and worldwide
Website and Social Media	• https://jackfruitmarketing.com/ • https://www.facebook.com/jackfruitmarketing • https://www.linkedin.com/company/jackfruit-marketing • https://twitter.com/JKassteen

From One Brand Evolves Many

An institution's brand is a mix of experiences, impressions, and beliefs. While staff, faculty, students, and alumni might each describe a brand differently, if done right, there will be at least one common thread woven throughout everyone's description. And that common thread is the unique value proposition on which a brand (institution) should capitalize.

Brand Moments

It is important to remember that while an official alumni ambassador (see chapter 4) may be formally recognized and trained by the institution, every other alum is a walking embodiment of that brand.

But where does a living, breathing brand begin? One could argue that the moment a prospect becomes a student signifies that the institution has accepted this person into its brand. The student has officially moved from being an outsider to becoming part of the institution's lifelong brand family. The role students play within that family will depend on their persona and the institution's efforts to nurture them into becoming engaged students and active alumni. The next critical moment in the journey—when a student graduates and becomes an alum—is the moment when institutions deem that he or she embodies their brand.

Becoming Part of a Brand

An interesting thing happens when a person moves from being a prospect to a student: The brand is internalized and becomes part of the student's identity. Until a student (and especially an international one who likely will not set foot on campus until Welcome Week) physically arrives at a university, the brand exists as a promise. Prospects experience snippets of this brand promise in every interaction they have with an institution—from social media posts to emails to receiving an acceptance letter—yet they do not truly fall into a brand until their student experience actually begins. For example, if students accept their place in the upcoming admissions cycle but then defer for a year, it is fair to say that these students are not wholly part of the institution's brand. They have yet to begin their studies, attend their first meeting of a student club, or embrace the institutional mascot. In other words, while they have received an invitation to the party, they have not yet arrived.

Having a physical presence on campus is a huge part of formulating the brand experience. The COVID-19 pandemic has forced every institution to reconsider how that experience is conveyed virtually, but it is also a useful example to showcase the effects that a physical detachment has on a brand. The college campus environment is designed to foster friendships, create memories, and occasionally take students out of their comfort zones, be it through academic challenges or cocurricular activities. Collectively, all of these micro-moments add up to formulate a unique brand experience, and as many institutions learned in 2020, the online experience is quite different from the physical one.

Institutions supporting traditional, in-person learning and living environments see this type of detachment and transition again when international students graduate and change status once more to become alumni. At this time, institutions bid farewell to new graduates, knowing they may never step foot on campus again. As the physical gap grows wider and more time passes, the link becomes more tenuous, and therefore the need to reinforce a brand connection becomes stronger.

So, just as institutions nurture newly accepted students in their transformations toward becoming graduates, colleges and universities must also nurture new alumni as their alma mater moves from being a provider and memory-maker to being a friend, partner, or even beneficiary.

Evolving the Brand

Institutions have been building their brand since day one, and it is now the alumni's turn to carry their brand into the world; however, this comes with some risk. Once a brand is out of an institution's influence and control, anything can happen. Every member of the alumni community is a walking embodiment of an institutional brand, but every person is different. And people are notoriously unpredictable.

When it comes to managing the institutional brand on an international scale, it is important to first acknowledge that there will be many aspects beyond the institution's control. Second, institutions will want to establish clear guidelines around acceptable brand deviations. For example, how important is it that others describe the institution as "highly ranked" versus "well ranked?" While they might have slightly different connotations, from a search engine optimization (SEO) perspective both terms are useful; therefore, this might illustrate an area of brand deviation that is acceptable.

This example also illustrates the consequences of user-generated content (UGC). An institutional brand is not a black-and-white, unbending object. Its core is solid, yet it takes different forms depending on who experiences the brand. It is natural that each student or alumni will describe a university slightly differently, and indeed, this variance can lead to newfound revelations for the brand or to a gradual brand evolution.

Institutions seeking UGC from alumni (e.g., stories, reviews, recommendations) will want to loosen their requirements to allow for slight deviations in the way the institutional brand is presented. This is a great opportunity for university departments to collaborate so that the integrity of the brand remains intact; meanwhile, each division can simultaneously acquire and share different brand representations from various audiences. For example, the admissions department can use specific UGC with student personas during the recruitment process, and student services might use alternative UGC with students at orientation or in a counseling session. Additionally, the career center can leverage alumni UGC when encouraging students to explore internships or when preparing them for job interviews. UGC obtained from older alumni can be shared with younger alumni as inspiration, support, or guidance.

Brand Connections

Strong brands create connections with prospects and lasting relationships with students and alumni. The good news is that institutions have already started doing this; students likely have been exposed to the institution's brand for months or years before enrollment, and alumni experienced the brand directly during their time as students. The challenge is to maintain that relationship for life. To do so requires more than monthly newsletters or networking events. It requires adopting an intentional, strategic focus on two-way engagement, creating ongoing experiences for each stage of the alumni life cycle, and fulfilling the needs of alumni throughout their personal and professional journeys.

First Impressions Paying Dividends in Graduate Programs

One never gets a second chance to make a first impression, and perception is reality. These truisms are well understood in higher education marketing circles as institutions devote more resources to creating the strongest and most immediate connections with prospective students. As research shows (Gibbons 2018; Wargo 2006), first impressions are made within seconds of the initial interaction, whether it be in person or virtually. Strong first impressions are particularly important for shorter programs such as graduate degrees, where international students will have brief on-campus experiences. It is vital in these programs that international students feel a connection early on in their academic careers, and even before starting their coursework.

> CASE STUDY

Graduate Connections: Fordham University Law School's Master's Program
Adapted from an interview with Toni Jaeger-Fine (2020)

Institution	Fordham Law School
Motto	In the service of others
Founded	1905
Location	New York City (Manhattan)
Number of Students in 2020	1,549 (approximately 8% of which are international)
Number of Alumni in 2020	22,080
Department Responsible for International Alumni Relations	Office of Alumni Relations
Alumni Relations Office Website	https://www.fordham.edu/info/20636/school_of_law_alumni

Graduate programs, just like undergraduate programs, frequently engage their international alumni to build greater name recognition around the world. Fordham University in New York City partners with its growing international alumni cohort from the nine masters in law (LLM) programs currently offered by the law school. The LLM program celebrated its 30th anniversary in 2019 and marked the occasion with a special event featuring a Colombian alum who received her undergraduate law and first master's degree in France as a keynote speaker.

Fordham LLM programs attract on average 150 students, of which 90 to 95 percent are international. No one country or region predominates; the students hail from Africa, Asia, Europe, Latin America, and the Middle East. Some students receive financial aid, and program officers have not historically relied on the alumni for donations.

"Development opportunities are not as great from [former] international students, compared to domestic students," confides assistant dean Toni Jaeger-Fine. However, Jaeger-Fine acknowledges an even greater opportunity: "The greatest thing I can gain from alumni are referrals. When an alum talks positively about the program, it is gold."

Fordham's LLMs are one-year programs, so the opportunity to build a relationship with students is much shorter compared to the opportunities during undergraduate degrees or other graduate programs such as medicine. "First impressions count," Jaeger-Fine says. "The impression you make has to be immediate and genuine so that everyone feels welcomed and supported."

Having easily accessible and updated information about the LLM programs and ways to inquire about admission is important to retain credibility as a responsive institution. Moreover, having a live interaction with an informed person can contribute to an immediate positive impression. International alumni are some of the most informed ambassadors for their alma mater. For the international LLM alumni, professional contacts are incredibly important, so access to the alumni network is one of the major benefits for staying involved and engaged.

"Our LLM students are making an enormous financial and life decision to come to Fordham, and they want to know they have a point person to turn to. With all the cultural and linguistic differences, students find comfort knowing there are personal resources," Jaeger-Fine says. According to focus groups with LLM students, 9 out of 10 chose Fordham because of the personal touch. "There are few schools that can stand alone on their reputation; beyond that, little differences in the things we do can set us apart from others."

The LLM program facilitates relationships between the alumni and student communities, which gives the students the feeling that Fordham's global network of legal professionals around the world is invested in student success. One example of this took place in 2020, when the program organized a virtual alumni careers panel for current and prospective LLM students, domestic and international, with their alumni based in New York City. After graduation, many students are interested in staying and working in New York City, one of the most dynamic legal markets in the world. At the end of every presentation, the alumni made the same generous offer to the participants: "Feel free to reach out to me."

Jaeger-Fine and her colleagues see programs such as the virtual alumni careers panel as key marketing tools for the future. "We did this live in the past, but this is one area that is easier for everyone to get on Zoom. It's less of an ask, schedules are more fluid, and no one has to navigate New York City traffic."

Recent Graduates as Young International Alumni Ambassadors

Alumni relations professionals often wonder how they can boost international alumni chapters while engaging with young international alumni, former international students who have graduated within the past 2 years. Benefits of engaging recent graduates as international alumni ambassadors include (1) opportunities for senior, more established alumni to connect with newer alumni; (2) the ability to meet sustainability goals, such as mentoring and chapter leadership succession planning; and (3) recognition for young alumni that can incentivize further involvement. Finally, young international alumni ambassador programs help establish intergenerational affinity to the homeland, alma mater, and international communities.

Young alumni are typically active social media users and hold a powerful seat of influence that can be leveraged by institutions that invest in developing their relationships with these recent graduates. Young alumni who feel their relationship with their alma mater brings them personal and professional value may remain open to an ongoing dialogue, in person or virtually. The value proposition increases when institutions engage international young alumni who are interested in volunteer leadership roles that can be developed and executed no matter where they live or work. These leadership positions are ways for recent graduates to develop communication skills and transferrable work experience through ongoing contact with more experienced alumni and to enhance their résumés as this commitment demonstrates that their alma mater trusts them to represent its brand.

Northeastern University's Young Global Leaders program exemplifies the value of recent graduates and their alma mater maintaining productive, two-way relationships.

Chapter 6

CASE STUDY

A Learning Opportunity for Young Leadership: Northeastern University

Adapted from an interview with Carolyn Jasinski, MA (2020)

Institution	Northeastern University
Motto	*Lux, veritas, virtus* (Light, truth, courage)
Founded	1898
Location	Boston, Massachusetts, with regional campuses in Portland, Maine; Charlotte, North Carolina; Seattle, Washington; and San Francisco Bay Area, California; Toronto and Vancouver, Canada; and London, United Kingdom
Number of Students in 2020	19,462 undergraduate students (16% of which are international) 9,846 graduate students (59% of which are international)
Number of Alumni in 2020	More than 275,000 alumni in 177 countries (9% of which live outside of the United States)
Department Responsible for International Alumni Relations	Alumni Relations/University Advancement
Alumni Relations Office Website	alumni.northeastern.edu

In 2011, a graduating senior sent a proposal to Northeastern University President Joseph E. Aoun. His idea? To launch an international network of young alumni volunteers for Northeastern, suggesting recent graduates could carry elements of their on-campus student leadership experiences into their alumni careers. This new organization would also enable international alumni to meet and stay in touch with other like-minded graduates who care about fostering a strong global brand for their alma mater.

Aoun eagerly lent his support and officially appointed the first cohort with guidance from the student founder. Thus, the Young Global Leaders (YGL) program was born. After the first cohort, members were identified from various sources, including self-nomination, faculty recommendations, YGL peer recommendations, and regional community leader recommendations. YGL continues to be one of the most successful examples of international alumni engagement at Northeastern.

Membership

YGL is a "next generation" international leadership community, which means that it builds a pipeline of future Northeastern leaders. Members come from countries around the world, representing every corner of the global network that is important to the university's strategy. Members are under 35 years of age and, after crossing over this threshold, they move to a lifetime membership. Typically, 120 members are active in any given year, and participation includes a minimum annual leadership gift to the YGL Fund, which is a collective gift fund (see the "Donations" section).

YGL programs help to connect networks around the globe. By marketing events and initiatives to current international students, YGL members bring together active international student leaders with alumni members. Carolyn Jasinski, executive director of leadership relations and advancement initiatives, confirms the importance of including all global markets as YGL members. "If a YGL volunteer from Guatemala leaves, then the group will ensure it recruits a new leader from that country," says Jasinski. "Our network of Young Global Leaders helps to source new members from their outreach efforts in their respective countries."

Responsibilities

YGL members carry out a variety of roles. Members serve as advisory representatives in areas such as entrepreneurship, global employer relations, and the university's Global Perspective Series and Summits. YGL members also carry out traditional volunteer roles in their home countries and regions; they actively support international student recruitment as college fair hosts and participants on career panels (see page 124), attend alumni relations events, recruit mentors, and source hosts for international co-op job placements. All of these roles are even more vital when normal travel and outreach are prevented.

Unlike some boards, YGL does not have any governing or fiduciary responsibilities; rather, members are recognized for their abilities to connect, influence, and reach audiences around the world where they work and live. Members meet annually with the university leadership team, including the president. During a yearly Global Leadership Summit, the university turns to its YGL "insiders" to inform its international networks.

"The cultural understanding—how Northeastern needs to communicate its messaging with local context—is critical," Jasinski emphasizes. "As an example, members tell us when it's a good time to schedule in-country engagements to attain the widest reach."

In 2020, the university called on all YGL members to step up their involvement to support current students and assist with international student orientation in the Northeastern network. Jasinski recalls, "Travel barriers have not stopped the busy pace. Members we have never met in person are now meeting online. With everyone staying in one place, we have greater access to thought leadership and no barriers to connecting our networks."

Donations

YGL members convene once a year, rotating to different countries, and their sessions often align with those of the university trustees. During these meeting, they learn about current university priorities, including the university's philanthropic goals. A democratic voting process decides how members designate their annual gift from the YGL Fund. Members are not asked to solicit peer-to-peer donations, but have been influential in matching potential international investors from their home country to specific funding needs identified by trustees, the president, and other officials, and establishing funds that back the ideas sourced from their networking efforts. The program celebrated its 10th anniversary in 2021, and the network's commitment to Northeastern remains constant.

International Travel as a Brand Management Tool

Alumni can be the eyes, ears, and voice of an institution. Well-informed alumni motivated to support the institution can strengthen its reputation around the world as they travel, especially when they connect with a community. International travel programs are an investment in alumni and their experiences, both individual and collective, that can serve the institution as well.

CASE STUDY

How to Make the Most of International Alumni Group Travel
By Kathy Edersheim, MBA

Business Name	Impactrics, LLC
Motto	Strengthening education through enhanced alumni engagement supported by powerful metrics
Mission	Providing the tools and guidance, including robust, customized metrics, to develop and deliver strong alumni relations programs to benefit the institution, the students, the alumni, and the broader community
Founded	2017
Locations	New York, global
Website and Social Media	• Impactrics.com • https://www.linkedin.com/company/impactrics

Recognizing the importance of international alumni to the alumni relations effort is a first step in building long-term connections. Understanding that opportunities for international engagement are deep and fulfilling is the next step.

While COVID-19 led to a hiatus, in the long run, we live in an age of travel. In 2019, more money was spent on leisure travel than ever before (Lock 2020). To meet the growing international interest, universities can (and do) offer educational or affinity travel opportunities to their alumni. For example, a university might offer a trip designed for alumni and friends to a historically important site such as Machu Picchu, hosted by a professor of Incan history. The purpose of these organized travel opportunities is generally a blend of engagement with the university and revenue generation. Revenue can come from pricing in a profit margin, being paid commission by a travel operator, or receiving donations from appreciative travelers before or after the trip. It is no surprise that those who can afford to be travelers are likely to be donors and to give again, perhaps at a higher level, after a trip. And most institutions have found that the trips generate loyalty. Depending on the institution, statistics show that 35 to 65 percent of travelers on alumni trips join another trip in the future, so one of the best prospects for a trip is someone who has traveled with the institution before (DelliPriscoli and Edersheim 2019).

Beyond educational travel, there are types of trips that can provide a deeper and more impact-driven type of engagement for alumni and the sponsoring institution: mission- and service-based programs. These programs call on alumni to gather and work together—perhaps facilitating a summer program in Alaska or building a house in Mexico—often near spectacular sites that can be visited on the same trip. As members of a group organized by the university, these participants are brand ambassadors to the partnering communities around the world. By calling on alumni to volunteer as part of a delegation consisting of other alumni, family, and friends from around the world, a deep and enduring bond can be formed with others on the trip and members of the hosting community. The participants will appreciate the institution for providing the opportunity and structure for the fulfilling experience.

But what about future engagement with the institution beyond participation in another trip? Group travel of all sorts is ideal for building community among alumni. Travelers demonstrate a shared interest in a topic or destination and in being part of a group. The trip provides a foundation of a shared experience. The trip leader, whether lecturer, host, or organizer, threads the institution's identity and branding throughout the trip. The bonding experience, shared interest, and identity from the institution are the key components of a strong alumni bond and community. Groups from a trip often organize their own "mini reunions" or plan their next excursion together.

From the institution's perspective, travel provides a unique opportunity for the faculty leader or staff representative, such as an alumni officer, to learn about the participants and the ways that they want to engage beyond their demonstrated interest in travel. Each trip is fertile ground for fostering engagement around the institutional mission with discussions, updates, and activities, such as alumni gatherings in a destination city. It might take some additional planning and different preparation to generate engagement, but it is likely to be well worth it.

After any travel program that has brought alumni together for many days for a deeply meaningful experience, there should be follow-up with the travelers to discuss additional engagement possibilities based on their interests and expertise. Upon returning from the trip, the trip leader, usually a staff member or sometimes a volunteer, should provide information to the institution's volunteer management and development teams so that the right person can follow up to discuss the potential for all types of gifts and engagement.

Multiple Affinities and Managing Brand and Reputation

So far, this chapter has covered ways that alumni can support a single institution's brand. However, sometimes alumni have multiple affinities or brands that they can promote. In the publication *Staying Global: How International Alumni Relations Advances the Agenda*, Tania Schwartz and Gretchen Dobson (2015, 98) write about the notion of "multiple affinities" and provide several examples that challenge the notion of alumni relations as a "one-to-one relationship between a single university and its graduates." With the advances in online learning, the expanding middle class in developing countries, and an overall consumer mentality of enterprising students wanting to maximize the value of their diploma, a growing number of international alumni have taken courses or completed parts of their degrees at several universities, often in different countries. The value of an international degree from two or more institutions and how that impacts one's sense of employability are primary factors driving student recruitment.

Aalto University in Finland, an example of multiple affinities, is a story of three universities (Helsinki School of Economics, Helsinki University of Technology, and the University of Art and Design Helsinki) merging to create one educational institution that leverages strengths in the arts, science, technology, and business to provide cross-disciplinary academic programs. Schwartz and Dobson (2015) recall Aalto's story in relation to alumni with multiple affinities and suggest this example may be compared with the experience of multiple institutions cooperating internationally. The example may also apply to domestic institutions preparing to manage local mergers or start a new partnership with another institution. Three takeaways emerged.

Chapter 6

CASE STUDY
Arriving at a Common Identity: Aalto University
By Gretchen Dobson, EdD

Institution	Aalto University
Motto	Towards a Better World
Founded	2010
Location	Helsinki, Finland
Number of Students in 2019	5,869 undergraduates (4% of which are international) 5,337 master's students (25% of which are international)
Number of Alumni in 2019	45,000 alumni from more than 80 countries
Department Responsible for International Alumni Relations	Alumni Relations
Alumni Relations Office Website	https://www.aalto.fi/en/for-alumni

Align Mission and Brand

Aalto knew attempting to engage an expanded alumni base might affect the relationship of alumni to their original institutions that no longer exist under their original names nor operate individually. The institution spoke from an "Aalto alumni" perspective from the very beginning and marketed this new expanded alumni network as an opportunity to create multidisciplinary encounters. In the case of collaborations between institutions, a strategic communications plan to students, alumni, faculty, and other key stakeholders can include the value of a community aligned under one mission.

Reassess Data Management

Expanded networks result in expanded databases and require adopting an existing or new customer relationship management (CRM) platform and agreeing on consistent procedures for capturing and reporting alumni data, such as alumni activity. Universities in the exploratory stages of a potential merger or partnership can take initial steps to outline their international dataset management practices and assess which existing practices have been most effective and which practices are not recommended.

Find a Middle Ground

While Aalto created an umbrella that offers multidisciplinary services, alumni are still connected to their original university identities and alumni networks, which provide services and focus their messaging and participation goals from the university and field of study perspectives. This combination of convergence and divergence has worked well for all involved. The level of connectedness can vary across institutions and be one of the main ways alumni want to affiliate. Awareness of these differences can help institutions target their engagement strategies.

Ambassador Programs Across States, Territories, and Provinces

As is the case with Aalto, there have been growing efforts to combine alumni engagement efforts across countries or regions to create a cohesive strategy. This is the case in Australia, where states and territories recognize the value of maintaining relationships with international alumni.

Data suggest about 85 percent of international students depart Australia after their studies (Treasury and Department of Home Affairs 2018). Many of these alumni go on to become influential in all walks of life and have the potential to contribute to trade relations, research, investment, and other valuable benefits for states, territories, and nations.

In Australia, states and territories sponsor programs to promote trade and investment and boost economic and industry development. Defined focus areas include collaboration with government, industry, and research institutions; stakeholders—like international alumni—have been asked to contribute to improved outcomes for business, industry, and the community, both at home and abroad. A state- or territory-wide international alumni ambassador program can help establish an engaged community of international alumni who graduated from one of the state's or territory's registered education providers to serve as ambassadors for the respective region.

State- and territory-wide international alumni ambassador initiatives not only showcase the region as a study destination but also support the state or territory's broader industry, trade, and investment agenda. States and territories may want to invite select education providers to cosponsor these initiatives. Two models, student ambassadors and mid-career ambassadors, engage different types of international alumni, but both serve an overriding objective of increasing brand awareness.

Student Ambassadors

The first concept leverages the involvement of an engaged set of international students who have served as student ambassadors. These types of programs provide personal and professional development and networking opportunities to the state, territory, or province's "rising stars" who are recruited across all education providers within the region. International student ambassadors are actively involved in promotional and marketing campaigns and practice their new skills as spokespersons. Upon graduation, international student ambassadors interested in remaining involved with international students, their former providers, and the international education sector become alumni ambassadors.

Specifically, an international student alumni ambassador program has the potential to realize the following objectives:

States, Territories, and Provinces
- Promote international education and training opportunities in the region.
- Provide insider information to visiting ministerial or trade delegations.

Education Providers
- Promote the region as a study destination.
- Help providers build their international outreach.
- Spread institutional brands.
- Boost promotional channels.
- Establish more networks to support alumni and student employment.
- Enhance relationships between alumni's alma mater(s) in the region.

Participating and Prospective International Student Ambassador Alumni
- Grow personal and professional networks and engage with fellow regional alumni.
- Learn about investment opportunities between the host region, home region, and other professional stakeholders.
- Gain opportunities to showcase their professional profiles in print and electronic publications and on social media sites.

Mid-Career Ambassadors

The second international alumni ambassador concept is distinct in mobilizing former international undergraduate and graduate students who have left their state, territory, province, or country and are now mid-career professionals (i.e., 10–15 years post-study). Waiting at least a decade to engage these alumni has a two-pronged effect: (1) It gives alumni time to attain workplace success, and (2) it helps institutions identify potential leaders, as early career achievements are an effective indicator of future leadership and giving potential (EAB 2016). Working together with their respective institutions, a state, territory, or province may develop cohorts of alumni based on industry expertise or interest in other public diplomacy initiatives related to strengthening bilateral partnerships and people-to-people linkages.

These strategies fall under the alumni ambassador category since the program's aim is to build a corps of international experts with strong personal and professional ties to the respective region or country. In short, these strategies endeavor to engage small cohorts of influential alumni who will participate in high-level engagement events and advance the interests of the state.

Conclusion

Brand and reputation are enhanced through strong relationships with engaged international alumni. The way the brand of a school, city, state, or country is perceived will vary, and the deployment of international alumni ambassador programs is one way education providers may manage perceptions, messages to stakeholders, and how they conduct their business overseas. Institutions without strong international alumni engagement strategies lose brand promotion opportunities, especially when vying for the attention of prospective students in new or emerging markets. As the examples in the next section support, having a strong international alumni engagement strategy provides a competitive advantage in attracting and recruiting talent, as international students rank brand highly in their decision-making.

References

DelliPriscoli, J. Mara, and Kathy Edersheim. 2019. *Insights into the Educational Affinity Travel Market*. Educational Travel Consortium. https://educationaltravel.travel/resources/.

EAB. 2016. "Help Your Mid-Career Alumni Evolve into Engaged Philanthropists." July 7. https://eab.com/insights/expert-insight/advancement/help-your-mid-career-alumni-evolve-into-engaged-philanthropists/.

Gibbons, Serenity. 2018. "You and Your Business Have 7 Seconds to Make a Good First Impression: Here's How to Succeed." *Forbes.* June 19. https://www.forbes.com/sites/serenitygibbons/2018/06/19/you-have-7-seconds-to-make-a-first-impression-heres-how-to-succeed/?sh=7648781056c2.

Jaeger-Fine, Toni. 2020. Interview by Gretchen Dobson. August 20, 2020.

Jasinski, Carolyn. 2020. Interview by Gretchen Dobson. September 1, 2020.

Lock, S. 2020. "Global Tourism Industry—Statistics & Facts." Statista, December 9. https://www.statista.com/topics/962/global-tourism/.

Schwartz, Tania, and Gretchen Dobson. 2015. "International Alumni with Multiple Affinities." In *Staying Global: How International Alumni Relations Advances the Agenda*, ed. Gretchen Dobson. EAIE Occasional Paper 24.

Sofiri. 2020. "Digital Marketing Trends in International Student Recruitment." Sofiri (blog). August 2. https://sofiri.com/blog/digital-marketing-trends-in-international-student-recruitment/.

Toyn, Gary W. 2020. *The Alumni Relations Benchmarking Study: Voluntary Alumni Engagement in Support of Education.* Alumni Access. https://f.hubspotusercontent00.net/hubfs/263750/Alumni_Access_VAESE_Study%202020_VF.pdf.

Treasury and the Department of Home Affairs. 2018. *Shaping a Nation: Population Growth and Immigration Over Time.* Commonwealth of Australia. https://research.treasury.gov.au/sites/research.treasury.gov.au/files/2019-08/Shaping-a-Nation-1.pdf.

Wargo, Eric. 2006. "How Many Seconds to a First Impression?" Association for Psychological Science. July 1. https://www.psychologicalscience.org/observer/how-many-seconds-to-a-first-impression.

Attracting and Retaining Talent

Of the many ways alumni engage with their alma mater, assisting with international student recruitment has never been more important and timely. Concerted efforts have been made to onboard international and transnational alumni to serve as marketing and recruitment volunteers and, in some instances, highly engaged international alumni ambassadors. International alumni have played an active role in advancing international student mobility, as evidenced over the past decade across undergraduate, graduate, and short-term educational programs.

International alumni initiatives may originate from different points within an institutional organizational chart, most often from the international office or the alumni and advancement offices. A 2017 benchmarking study by Intead and Academic Assembly, Inc. (Andrews and Mattern 2017) surveyed 97 U.S. colleges, universities, and other postsecondary institutions about their current international alumni management practices, their rating of the programs' consistency and effectiveness, their areas of frustration, and how much value they and their institutional leadership ascribe to the work of international alumni development. More than 50 percent of respondents reported feeling that international alumni management was "very important" to increasing international student recruitment and brand awareness, but nearly 30 percent of the sample did not feel they received sufficient internal leadership support. A key recommendation from the study asserted the value of starting small and demonstrating success as a means of building links within the institution as well as the buy-in of institutional leaders.

This chapter highlights examples of how international alumni serve as vital partners in attracting interest and retaining talent across a variety of institutions and how support from institutional leadership has enhanced these efforts. It begins with actionable tips for building effective international alumni recruitment models gleaned from a U.S. university, followed by Wilfrid Laurier University's story of how a collaborative relationship between the alumni relations and international student recruitment units has created an active international recruiting environment. Next, the University of New England describes the benefits of embracing peer-to-peer online platforms for attracting prospective students who gain valuable perspectives from current international students and alumni. Northeastern University provides an example of a virtual international alumni career panel that supports international student recruitment. The chapter concludes with an in-depth look at how an international alumni relations program from Central European University manages alumni involvement through key investments made over time to sustain commitment.

CASE STUDY

Five Tips for Building Effective International Alumni Recruitment Models

Adapted from an interview with Aaron Zdawczyk (2020)

Institution	Northwestern University
Motto	*Quaecumque sunt vera* (Whatsoever things are true)
Founded	1851
Location	Evanston, Illinois
Number of Students in 2020	8,327 undergraduates (10% of which are international)
Number of Alumni in 2020	More than 200,000
Responsible Department for International Alumni Relations	Alumni Relations
URL of Alumni Relations Office	alumni.northwestern.edu

Experienced international student recruitment professionals like Northwestern University's Aaron Zdawczyk, senior associate director of admission and director of recruitment strategy and initiatives, can tell stories about being the only recruitment officer representing their institution around the world. For more than a decade, Zdawczyk built relationships with prospective students, families, and international alumni. As he grew his career with Northwestern, he expanded his personal relationships with key colleagues with direct interest in international alumni relations and began developing a way to connect the dots to support the recruitment cycle and Northwestern's ongoing efforts to grow its reputation abroad. He says, "This includes building the relationships in person and understanding the dynamics of the local environment. In the last five years, we made some massive shifts in how we engage alumni. A lot of our growth was due to internal changes we made to how our admissions, alumni, and international offices worked together."

The positive changes have brought to light some enduring lessons. Zdawczyk points to five considerations when building effective international alumni recruitment models:

1. **Recruitment is a team sport:** Form partnerships with other departments and determine shared programmatic goals. Commit to practicing clear and effective communication between the staff member who leads international recruitment, admissions staff who work with alumni, and other offices that engage with alumni.
2. **Recruiting a representative alumni base matters:** Consider the recruitment market demographics and how alumni who match those demographics—and have access to prospective students—can build effective relationships locally. The institution should consider the impact of this selection on the community and culture.
3. **Develop the playbook:** Publish a digital international alumni student recruitment handbook for volunteers.

> **Recommended Topics for Volunteer Handbooks**
> - Professional conduct and standards
> - Calendar of responsibilities
> - How to stay connected and up to date
> - Ways to be involved
> - Contact information for admissions and other relevant offices
> - Explanations of application and selection processes
> - Explanation of financial aid or assistance programs
> - Statistical breakdown of incoming class and overall student body
> - Interview procedures and samples or case studies (if relevant)
> - Institutional overview, mission, and priorities
> - International student support and services
> - Answers to frequently asked questions

4. **Reward the MVPs:** Developing a system for ongoing or seasonal recognition motivates volunteers to remain active and energized. Consider categories such as greatest number of interviews conducted in a season and service milestones such as five-year anniversaries.
5. **Forecast challenges and plan accordingly:** Before engaging with alumni, admissions offices should carefully review potential problems and decide how to best address them within their institutional culture. For example, know which social media platforms are restricted in which countries, and develop protocols and policies around compliance, data privacy, and types of access alumni may be given in their official roles.

The shift to virtual recruitment and more limited interaction with international alumni volunteers during the COVID-19 pandemic prompted Zdawczyk's team to add more training resources to support the alumni who were organizing the volunteers in each country or region. Resources included videos and documents that were culturally sensitive to the impact of the pandemic on international students and their families. The success of this strategy was in part due to a conscious effort to use YouTube as a place to record and publish information that the team wanted different target markets to consume, including alumni volunteers. Content was recorded in advance, published according to a predetermined schedule, and categorized to enhance search engine optimization.

Across the alumni and admissions areas, the staff are working on what they can do to make the international alumni experience better. There is a conscious effort to encourage more interaction between alumni volunteers who support recruitment and those volunteers engaged more broadly with the Northwestern Alumni Association and to develop more international recruitment alumni leaders to provide a global perspective to annual planning processes.

Zdawczyk sums up some final considerations: "International alumni engagement is not a one-size-fits-all model. Investment in resources must be based on where we can grow and build a sense of community, and where we can provide a space for alumni to interact."

Collaboration with the International Student Recruitment Team

Wilfrid Laurier University's international alumni and recruitment story is one of shared values, internal collaboration, careful planning, and solid stewardship of international alumni resources. This case study illustrates how collaboration between alumni relations and international recruitment units can benefit the goals of each.

CASE STUDY

How Collaborative Communities Advance Recruitment and Alumni Engagement Success: Wilfrid Laurier University
By Christie Johnson and Brittany Russell, MEd

Institution	Wilfrid Laurier University
Motto	Inspiring lives of leadership and purpose
Founded	1911
Location	Waterloo and Brantford, Ontario, Canada
Number of Students in 2020	21,586 (8% of which are international)
Number of Alumni in 2020	109,213 (4% of which live internationally outside of Canada)
Department Responsible for International Alumni Relations	Alumni Relations
Alumni Relations Office Website	www.laurieralumni.ca

Wilfrid Laurier University (Laurier) is a public university in Ontario, Canada, with four campuses across the country; the flagships are located in Waterloo and Brantford. In fall 2011, the university recruited 114 international students (more than 70 percent from China), and for fall 2020, the number of incoming international students grew to 427, representing 42 countries.

Starting Off Solo: Engaging International Alumni in Recruitment Efforts

Christie Johnson, the manager of international recruitment and partnerships, started working with international alumni before forming a relationship with the alumni office. To date, the university does not have a comprehensive internationalization strategy, but it does exhibit a commitment to serving international students, alumni, and other stakeholders. The International Recruitment unit has its own strategic plan and, working closely with the International Student Support and Global Engagement Offices, provides mobility services and support for international students and outreach to alumni and families. These recruitment efforts were augmented by current international students and alumni.

When Johnson started with International Recruitment, she hired international student ambassadors to help with recruitment events, such as open houses, and the ambassadors volunteered to assist with fairs overseas. International Recruitment realized it could stay in touch with these young alumni after graduation and continue to engage them on an international level. Johnson worked off the lists of international alumni provided by the alumni office, and she soon learned how helpful alumni of all ages could be—and wanted to be! Whether it was an alum who graduated 25 years ago who was a senior government official or more recent graduates, the influx of help was encouraging. Alumni wanted to receive updates on what was happening at Laurier; some joined the university at fairs; some collaborated on high school presentations; and some met with prospective students.

Paving the Way for Collaboration Between the Alumni and International Recruitment Units

Later, Brittany Russell was hired as alumni relations officer in the Alumni Relations Office. Over time, she found a way to attract budget for international alumni relations, paving the way for collaboration between the Alumni Relations and International

Recruitment units. The groundwork to gain these funds included (1) acquiring data on where International Recruitment traveled as well as the institution's alumni, and (2) sharing statistics with senior leadership about where international alumni were located. However, developing a strategic plan was reflective of years of collaborating and consistent adapting of processes to support the needs of both departments.

Year 1: Both units developed a list of international recruitment travel opportunities.

Year 2: The units learned more about each other's work, including the recruitment cycle and opportunities for collaboration.

Year 3: Members of the International Recruitment team joined Alumni Relations events outside of Ontario, and prospective students and parents were invited to join.

Year 4: The teams worked together to set goals for future programming and established the Global Ambassador Program (see page 121).

Throughout this time, the Alumni Relations and International Recruitment offices held regular meetings to share information, propose initiatives, and discuss ways to correspond with the alumni and track the communications.

Overcoming Data Challenges

When Russell started at Laurier in 2015, she understood that the lists of international alumni contact information were constantly changing and would require updating for the information to be as helpful as possible for the International Recruitment team's efforts. However, once she gained a better understanding of the goals of International Recruitment's trips, she was able to work with the Advancement Division's Prospect Research team to describe upcoming trips. The Prospect Research team is in a position to research alumni who live in those locations, where they work, and their time at Laurier (e.g., sports teams, campus clubs). Now that International Recruitment and Alumni Relations knew more about each other's travel schedules and the potential for working together, they were able to proactively request that the Prospect Research team look into alumni living in a specific city months in advance of any travel. This might mean updating a list of alumni who live in the area with business information or reviewing alumni databases to ensure information was correct. Once Alumni Relations received the updated list, it would flag for the International Recruitment team any alumni who had a relationship with Laurier staff from previous work, identified as a teacher or principal, or was a past student ambassador working in the area. These types of flags would help turn the cold ask of meeting with an alum into a warm one.

By researching professional positions and past involvement with Laurier, the teams were able to prioritize how they would approach alumni for the first time. For example, alumni who were high school principals could be a helpful resource to an International Recruitment officer for an upcoming trip.

Approaching International Alumni and Prospective Students

When approaching international alumni for the first time, Alumni Relations representatives acknowledged their Laurier educational background, their achievements since graduation, and how they may be able to help in the present. For the majority of alumni, it was the first time Laurier had reached out to them, outside of receiving campus updates via mail or email, and they were happy to assist the International Recruitment team overseas.

Alumni would come to meetings Laurier hosted with prospective students and families, sometimes to explain in their local language how Laurier teaches and supports students inside and outside the classroom, and sometimes to share their own experiences. Alumni also became knowledgeable about application requirements, such as the nuances between local and international curricula.

Within the year, Russell in Alumni Relations was able to negotiate the budget for the international piece of her role and continue to work with the International Recruitment team. Throughout the year, based on the admissions cycle, the teams would organize and pay for coffee, meals, or small alumni gatherings between alumni and the International Recruitment team. Sometimes there were 10 alumni around a table, and other times they were able to invite parents or prospective students. In some cases, current Laurier students on international co-op placements were invited to meet alumni. International Recruitment always packed Laurier-branded swag, like luggage straps, as well as current copies of the campus magazine and campus newspaper to thank alumni and share campus updates.

Falling into Stride Together

Now the teams have a solid formula for working together: International Recruitment shares its recruitment schedule and locations, and Alumni Relations organizes meetups and events with alumni and speakers.

The intentional working arrangement between Alumni Relations and International Recruitment has helped Laurier fulfill its diversity mandate. It has grown its international student numbers by 14 to 16 percent each year for the past 8 years—without any budget increases in that time.

Laurier has launched a new program called the Global Ambassador Program, composed of 29 alumni from around the world who want to stay connected to the university by volunteering as ambassadors. Laurier saw a need to make the Global Ambassador Program official after the successful launch of its first global day of service, Helping Hawks. When the institution began to look for community organizations to support the initiative, alumni and campus partners reached out with an organization in mind and interest in hosting other alumni for the volunteer day. Alumni were keen to continue supporting alumni engagement in their current home countries, which sparked the official launch of the Global Ambassador Program.

As Helping Hawks continues to grow, ambassadors have been able to host prospective students at the volunteer day so the latter can get to know alumni living in their area and ask questions in an informal setting. This type of involvement enables prospective students to get a feel for the campus culture by volunteering with alumni side by side.

The first international Helping Hawks events took place in Bermuda and China during a school break. Johnson joined alumni, current students, and prospective students for a beach cleanup in Bermuda. Prospective students learned about the Laurier community by spending time with the students and alumni.

Spawned by the success of the Global Ambassador Program, ambassadors host events throughout the year, meet with the International Recruitment team, and connect with the Laurier global alumni network. One ambassador reached out to share that her work was transferring her to London and that she wanted to connect with alumni who could help her better understand how to negotiate the tricky rental contracts. Another of the ambassadors shared that he moved from Dubai to Ireland to start an MBA program and has since met alumni in Ireland to help with his transition.

Sustaining Recruitment Priorities

A top priority for Laurier continues to be recruitment, both locally and globally. Any time International Recruitment staff write to a new international contact, they emphasize the theme of volunteering for Laurier around the world and how alumni are more than ready to lend a hand.

A new website for International Recruitment profiles ambassadors in key recruitment markets. The profiles focus on their academic and cocurricular experiences and how they feel their Laurier experience helped shape their personal development and career choices. The website also features a button that prompts prospective students to "Reach out to a Global Ambassador" to connect and ask questions. This generates an email to the ambassador and copies the international recruitment officer for that territory and Alumni Relations (a tip from coworkers from the University of Waterloo). If the ambassador is unable to respond to their queries, there is backup for one of the other contacts to respond. Laurier's internal collaboration has now been operationalized, the benefits optimized for both Alumni Relations and International Recruitment.

CASE STUDY

UNEBuddy Online Community of Influencers and Advocates: University of New England
Adapted from an interview with Alexandra Cook (2020)

Institution	University of New England
Motto	Out of wisdom comes moderation
Founded	1938
Location	Armidale, New South Wales, Australia
Number of Students in 2020	26,181 (7.3% of which are international)
Number of Alumni in 2020	128,759 (17% of which are international)
Departments Responsible for International Alumni Relations	Alumni Relations International Services
Alumni Relations Office Website	www.une.edu.au/alumni

The University of New England (UNE) in New South Wales, Australia, is a regional university with more than 25,000 students (approximately 21,000 studying online) and, of that, 1,400 international students (at peak times). Since 2018, UNE's international student recruitment office has partnered with online peer-to-peer networking provider UniBuddy to establish another way to reach prospective international students. The first cohort of buddies included both current undergraduate and graduate international students as well as academic and professional staff and has since grown to reach 30 to 40 profiles. The initial goals were to provide prospective students with resources and support in real time, and when international buddies could not answer a prospect's question about enrollment fees or visas, for instance, they could refer the question to their academic or staff UniBuddy peer.

In 2020, UNE rebranded UniBuddy to UNEBuddy. With student buddies graduating, the number of profiles decreased, and the program managers decided to add international alumni. This made sense for a few reasons: (1) With a small, one-person alumni relations office primarily focused on domestic alumni, inviting international alumni to join UNEBuddy could extend engagement; (2) UNE is a leader in online education, and alumni located all over the world could play a new role in recruitment; and (3) involving a new cohort of international alumni could lead to providing students additional online career and employability resources as well as future speakers for community programming.

The UNEBuddy program is selective. Two international alumni were recruited in July 2020 with a plan to develop six international alumni UNEBuddies by 2021. Alexandra Cook, international student engagement coordinator, explained, "We know our markets and proven strategy, so we'll handpick a couple of the international alumni after sending out an Expression of Interest. We need a cohort with a good mix of experience and educational interest. The good news is that since COVID-19, we have discovered that alumni across the world are keen to get involved with UNE and share their story."

Rebranding the program has produced new ways to motivate all the cohorts. The program has built in new incentives and monthly prizes for most engaged buddies and most creative blog posts, professional development opportunities, and invitations to seminars and online workshops, in addition to the small-scale UNEBuddy Awards designed to recognize top volunteers and thank all contributors.

Cook and colleagues from UNE's International Office have forged close and supportive relationships with the international student UNEBuddies. Upon graduation, these engaged students are welcome to continue their roles as international alumni buddies. As Cook sums up, "Our international students become our number-one ambassadors. They lend their voice and perspective in the recruitment process, and it makes sense to leverage and maintain these relationships."

Chapter 6

> **CASE STUDY**

Alumni Panels as Recruitment Events: Northeastern University
Adapted from an interview with Andre Kostousov, MBA (2020)

Institution	Northeastern University
Motto	*Lux, veritas, virtus* (Light, truth, courage)
Founded	1898
Location	Boston, Massachusetts, with regional campuses in Portland, Maine; Charlotte, North Carolina; Seattle, Washington; and San Francisco Bay Area, California; Toronto and Vancouver, Canada; and London, United Kingdom
Number of Students in 2020	19,462 undergraduate students (16% of which are international) 9,846 graduate students (59% of which are international)
Number of Alumni in 2020	More than 275,000 alumni in 177 countries (9% of which live outside of the United States)
Departments Responsible for International Alumni Relations	Alumni Relations/University Advancement
Alumni Relations Office Website	alumni.northeastern.edu

As Jacqueline Kassteen noted in the previous section on brand and reputation management, there is a great opportunity for university departments to collaborate so that the integrity of the institutional brand is consistently promoted while each division can achieve its own goals. An international alumni discussion panel that took place at Northeastern University in Boston, Massachusetts, in July 2020 exemplifies how the institution aligned its resources and thinking to find opportunities for various departments to support one another and leverage respective strengths.

By June 2020, international student recruitment for the following admissions cycle moved entirely online. To continue to build its international student pipeline, Northeastern's International Enrollment Management (IEM) Office took the lead in planning "Alumni Discussion Panel: Careers of the Future." Andre Kostousov, director of international enrollment strategies, conceived of the program by looking at hiring trends, the skills needed to fulfill positions, and how Northeastern is helping students develop those skills.

While the intended audience was prospective international students and the goal was to impact enrollment outcomes, Kostousov invited other university units to cosponsor the event, as there were specific roles for each area to play as well as direct benefits to their day-to-day operations, outlined in table 1.

Table 1. Alumni Discussion Panel Collaborators

Unit	Role	Benefit
Advancement	Recruit panelists	Furthers relationship-building with international alumni and donors
International Alumni Relations	Recruit panelists	Boosts international alumni participation and cultivates further volunteerism
School of Business	Have faculty members serve as moderators	Promotes school
Employer Engagement and Career Design	Recruit co-op employers for panel	Strengthens relationship with employer

The expert panel included senior executive panelists, three alumni, and one employer. One of the panelist was part of the Young Global Leaders program (see page 102). All were first-time volunteers. Two weeks prior to the panel, Kostousov held a training call with all the panelists so they could meet each other, hear others' stories and backgrounds, review the program, discuss talking points, and understand the program's desired outcomes.

The panel attracted more than 1,000 registrants, and on July 23, 2020, 350 attendees (primarily from India) logged on to participate. This was a 35 percent yield and a strong showing for the inaugural program.

From this first event, Kostousov extracted a few tips for strengthening future panels:
1. **Diversify the panel:** Recruit parents of current students or alumni who are internationally based, are leaders in their region or industries, and have experiences relevant to the topic of the panel. Involve university faculty and staff from appropriate knowledge areas as moderators and cohosts.

2. **Prepare with the moderator:** Select experienced and energetic facilitators who know how to ask questions, react, and extract interesting information from the panelists. Moderators should also do some research on the panelists so they know which questions to ask and understand the audience's motivations for attending. The success of panels depends on the moderator's ability to keep all engaged throughout the conversation.
3. **Choose technology wisely:** Technology sets the boundaries for what can happen (and what cannot) during a moderated virtual panel. Some platforms provide ways for small groups to break out into discussion rooms, which could be good for conversations between prospective students and alumni.

The alumni panel resulted in positive outcomes: The attending students took away insights about the institution, the panelists networked and built new connections, the IEM Office generated additional applications for admission, the other participating offices saw positive impacts on their respective relationships, and the university as a whole showcased its excellence, further contributing to advancing its reputation. This single event demonstrates the impact of effective collaboration, proper planning, and international alumni engagement on international student recruitment.

Mobilizing International Alumni Around Timely Events

International alumni chapters often sponsor programs to mobilize alumni around a timely activity or significant event. International student recruitment is both. The international marketing and recruitment cycle occurs at set times, and volunteers are needed at peak periods; programs such as accepted student receptions and predeparture orientations provide international chapters and alumni volunteer leaders a chance to build community among new students and families. The following example from Central European University elaborates on ways to motivate and provide ongoing support to international alumni volunteers and chapters, how approaches to international alumni engagement create opportunity and community, and how the university benefits from using an integrated volunteer management strategy.

CASE STUDY

Avenues for Alumni Engagement with Student Recruitment: Central European University
By Serge Sych, EdD

Institution	Central European University
Motto	Dare to make a difference
Founded	1991
Location	Vienna, Austria, and Budapest, Hungary
Number of Students in 2020	1,278 (81% of which are international)
Number of Alumni in 2020	17,749 (84% of which are international)
Department Responsible for International Alumni Relations	Alumni Relations Office
Alumni Relations Office Websites	• https://alumni.ceu.edu/ • https://alumni.ceu.edu/alumni-groups-worldwide

Central European University (CEU) was founded in 1991 to support the democratic transitions in Central and Eastern Europe and the former Soviet Union. Launching new undergraduate programs in 2020, CEU is now a global university with a focus on the social sciences and humanities. Campuses are based in Budapest and Vienna, with students from more than 100 countries and faculty from more than 50.

The CEU Alumni Volunteer Engagement Program was developed to meet the strategic needs of one of the most international institutions of higher education in the world. A four-pillar alumni engagement matrix includes (1) student recruitment, (2) career services, (3) local alumni groups, and (4) fundraising initiatives. Being a relatively young and small institution with an international student and alumni footprint (18,000 CEU alumni reside in nearly 150 countries), CEU needed a robust framework that could help the institution stay connected with alumni and reach a diverse global student recruitment market.

Mechanisms to Support and Motivate Volunteerism
The importance of international student recruitment has become a leverage for alumni relations and associated resource allocation within the institution. While keeping fundraising as an important element of the long-term alumni engagement

strategy, other areas such as career services and student recruitment have become flagship avenues for alumni engagement at CEU.

The following are examples of student recruitment events and communication functions supported by international alumni chapters and individual volunteers.

Connecting with Prospective and Admitted Students

CEU alumni volunteers provide references, share recruitment information, participate in the UniBuddy Connect project to engage with prospective students, represent CEU at educational fairs, and give presentations or host recruitment events for CEU. CEU relies on its alumni chapters and groups for organizing predeparture orientations for recently admitted students prior to their arrival at CEU. Alumni welcome the newly accepted students into the university community, providing them with first-hand information on the student experience while helping to boost institutional brand and increase enrollment yield.

Appealing to Academia

The Alumni in Higher Ed campaign aims to appeal to alumni working in academia who can promote the institution, share a recruitment web link, and use the alumni referral form, as well as appeal to academic partners to write letters of recommendation for applicants and recommend prospects directly to CEU programs. As part of CEU's high school outreach campaigns, alumni share their CEU experience at high school visits and fairs, an important influencing factor for younger students.

Maintaining Relationships with Recent Graduates

The Fresh Grads campaign engages CEU's recent graduates through tailored communication with call-to-action pitches. This group has proven to be very responsive in recruitment as soon as they join the alumni community. Fresh from CEU with recent memories and photos of their graduation ceremony, these graduates are the most enthusiastic and dynamic volunteers, who share (organically and by request) their graduation pictures as well as calls for applications and financial aid opportunities directly related to their affiliated communities (e.g., professional, academic, or demographic) via social media.

Generating Social Media Content

Alumni participate in social media outreach campaigns. These campaigns prominently feature alumni stories, posted via local alumni chapters on Facebook, Twitter, and Instagram during peak recruitment season.

Recruitment Support

Some of the key mechanisms that support recruitment activities include the following resources.

Expansive Networks

A worldwide network of more than 80 alumni chapters and clubs serves as a support framework for these programs. Prospects, applicants, and accepted students learn about CEU and its alumni network early on from community networking, information-sharing, and organized communication efforts by the university. Students are encouraged to connect with their local alumni groups to learn more about the CEU experience, get a sense of the CEU community, and explore future career prospects. Nearly one-third of accepted students heard about CEU from alumni or students, and the role of local alumni networks in building early connections with students is difficult to overstate.

Local Alumni Leaders

More than 120 leaders of alumni groups volunteer for their local alumni communities and support various recruitment and social functions at a city or national level. These recruitment activities include meetups with accepted students and predeparture orientations, which support student enrollment goals. The university annually coordinates and co-organizes with local alumni groups a range of events, including predeparture orientations in countries of new students' residence prior to their arrival at CEU. In 2019, 32 predeparture orientations took place, of which 13 were conducted online. Nearly 300 incoming students and 100 alumni participated. It is important to note that more students attended online events than in-person events, which proved particularly important in the context of the COVID-19 travel restrictions. (For a visual snapshot of orientation attendee demographics, see infogram.com/ceu-pdo-world-2019-1hdw2j9kzj3p6l0?live.)

Recruitment-Focused Alumni Volunteers

CEU has more than 30 dedicated alumni volunteers who specifically support student recruitment functions, as described in the "Alumni Recruitment Volunteers Terms of Reference" (see appendix 1). Many of them attend educational fairs, speak at schools and universities, and provide individual guidance to applicants as academic and professional references or mentors.

An Integrated Volunteer Management Approach

CEU's robust internal volunteer management program, designed by CEU staff, includes volunteer recruitment, training, stewardship, and recognition. These elements are integrated into a two-tier system (CEU n.d.) with Volunteer Pro and Volunteer Champion levels that recognize the quality and frequency of volunteers' engagement focusing on student recruitment. This program connects alumni relations with career services and enrollment management teams, all under auspices of the Office of the Vice President for Enrollment Management, Career Services, and Alumni Relations. While not common, such an integrated model has proven its efficiency by aligning a wide range of integral activities that follow students' journeys from prospects to alumni. Incoming classes consistently rate their interactions with alumni and enrolled students as the most important source of inspiration and information about CEU as their future study destination (about 30 percent).

Key Takeaways

1. Develop terms of reference and a job description for each alumni volunteer recruitment opportunity.
2. Involve alumni relations, career services, and enrollment management teams in developing an annual framework for volunteer management that includes volunteer recruitment, training, stewardship, and recognition.
3. Invest in the development of local alumni networks, and leverage their capacity so that formal or informal chapters and clubs become a global network of transnational student recruiters. These individuals are often the best storytellers and volunteers, providing all types of support needed on the ground, from organizing and participating in events to representing the institution at fairs and social gatherings with prospective and admitted students.
4. Engage alumni working in academia as volunteers by bridging their knowledge about higher education with their passion and support for their alma mater.

5. Develop social media outreach campaigns with the active involvement of alumni volunteers with large personal followings or active presence on their favorite platforms.

The investments in international alumni relations as integral to advancing international student recruitment is evident in CEU's comprehensive approach to international alumni relations, volunteer management, and training. Recognizing that some alumni self-identify as highly engaged—and being able to meet their interests and needs—is an important consideration for all involved in designing these recruitment programs.

Conclusion

Universities across the world are evaluating how they allocate finite resources to international marketing and student recruitment functions. Leveraging the interest, networks, and first-hand knowledge of international alumni is a proactive strategy for involving volunteers who desire to aid their alma mater in recruitment efforts. The best practices in this section make the case that the investment in international alumni relations programs can produce a rate of return that pays dividends for all involved.

References

Andrews, Cathryn, and Kate Mattern. 2017. "New Research: U.S. Global Alumni Management." *Intead* (blog). December 6. https://services.intead.com/blog/new-research-u.s.-global-alumni-management.

Central European University. 2019a. "PDOs by Attendance: People." Infogram. https://infogram.com/ceu-pdo-world-2019-1hdw2j9kzj3p6l0?live.

Central European University. 2019b. "Alumni Recruitment Volunteers Terms of Reference AY 2019–20." https://alumni.ceu.edu/sites/arcsdev.ceu.hu/files/attachment/basicpage/1881/studentrecruitmentvolunteers-tor2019.pdf.

Central European University. n.d. "CEU Alumni Volunteer Honor Roll." https://alumni.ceu.edu/ceu-alumni-volunteer-honor-roll.

Cook, Alexandra. 2020. Interview by Gretchen Dobson. July 29, 2020.

Kostousov, Andre. 2020. Interview by Gretchen Dobson. August 5, 2020.

Zdawczyk, Aaron. 2017. "Alumni Involvement in International Recruitment Initiatives." In *NAFSA's Guide to International Student Recruitment, Third Edition*, ed. Jessica Sandberg. Washington, DC: NAFSA: Association of International Educators.

Zdawczyk, Aaron. 2020. Interview by Gretchen Dobson. August 25, 2020.

Appendix 1

Central European University's Alumni Recruitment Volunteers Terms of Reference Academic Year (AY) 2019–20

Thank you for considering to join this very special group of alumni! As an alum, YOU are CEU's best asset to help recruit talented students from around the world. You can get involved with the Student Recruitment Office (STRO) in multiple ways.

What you can do:
- Refer people to CEU (e.g., faculty from other universities, youth organizations, companies)
- Share recruitment information about CEU and its programs (e.g., distributing brochures, calls for applications)
- Participate in the UniBuddy project to engage with prospective students
- Participate in STRO's social media campaigns (e.g., MyCEU, Instagram stories)
- Represent CEU at an educational fair
- Give presentations about CEU (e.g., at your home university, company)
- Organize or host a recruitment event for CEU (e.g., predeparture orientation)

How we recognize your efforts:
We have a two-tier system that recognizes **levels and frequency of engagement**.

Involvement level	Criteria
Level 1: Volunteer Pro	Refers min. 2 external partners to CEU/AY • Actively engages with prospective students in the UniBuddy project • Participates in min. 1 social media campaign/AY • Shares recruitment materials about CEU and its programs min. 3 times/AY
Level 2: Volunteer Champion	Engages in at least 2 of the following: • Participates in min. 1 education fair/AY • Organizes min. 1 presentation in their home country/AY • Hosts 1 predeparture orientation/AY

A **Volunteer Pro** fulfills at least one Level 1 criterion. A **Volunteer Champion** either fulfills at least two Level 2 criteria or volunteers with several CEU teams (Alumni Relations, Career Services, or Student Recruitment). For example, an active chapter contact who also volunteers as a recruitment volunteer is eligible to become Volunteer Champion for that academic year.

To maintain a level status, a volunteer has to remain active and fulfill the criteria for that particular level during an academic year. Existing volunteers will be reviewed and recognized for their contributions retroactively, based on their activity within the current academic year. Volunteer Champions will maintain their status for a grace period of one year, regardless of the level of their involvement.

What's in it for you?

- E-badges, updated each year (CEU Volunteer 2019, CEU Volunteer 2020, etc.), available to all volunteers
- Honor rolls of all volunteers on the ARO website
- Electronic holiday cards

When you reach the Volunteer Pro status:
- Volunteer spotlight article on the ARO website and in e-news
- Invitation to exclusive events, similar to donor and society member receptions
- Handwritten holiday cards
- CEU branded items to alumni speakers at career events, accompanied by thank-you cards/messages

When you reach the Volunteer Champion Status:
- Discounted tickets to the Reunion Gala
- Invitation to the President's reception during the Alumni Reunion Weekend
- Invitation to the annual Alumni Leadership Forum and public recognition during the event
- Shortlisting for the Alumni Impact Awards (Community Category)
- Access to select workshops and trainings for professional development and for increasing alumni volunteer potential

Employability for the Twenty-First Century

Recent global developments have led to job market disruptions; worldwide calls for greater inclusivity, equity, and social justice; and accelerated use of Fourth Industrial Revolution technologies. As the World Economic Forum (2018) explains:

> The Fourth Industrial Revolution is interacting with other socioeconomic and demographic factors to create a perfect storm of business model change in all industries, resulting in major disruptions to labour markets. New categories of jobs will emerge, partly or wholly displacing others. The skill sets required in both old and new occupations will change in most industries and transform how and where people work.

These disruptions are already bringing fundamental changes in the labor market, and international alumni networks can provide a safety net for students navigating through change. To help prepare students for postgraduation jobs, international alumni can serve as advisers, mentors, employers, and liaisons between the university and the public and private sectors. This section presents various ways that universities and organizations engage international alumni to help upgrade curricula, develop new competencies and skills, provide internships, open job opportunities, become mentors, and support global engagement and lifelong learning. It includes four examples from the field.

1. The Global Leadership Forum, a collaboration between Royal Melbourne Institute of Technology University and Common Purpose Student Experiences Limited, engages international alumni to inspire student leadership.

2. Sabancı University alumni prepare students to succeed in the tech industry.
3. Erasmus University Rotterdam facilitates an award-winning mentoring program that connects dedicated alumni volunteers worldwide to students through an online platform.
4. Universidad ESAN offers recent graduates opportunities to participate in programs at partner universities abroad, creating occasions for lifelong learning.

Curricula, Competencies, and Skills

To thrive in the twenty-first-century labor market, students must be able to manage change, maintain balance in unfamiliar situations, participate in lifelong learning, and reinvent their career paths many times (Harari 2019, 262). To help students be job-ready for the future, universities should explicitly teach critical thinking, problem-solving, effective communication, collaboration, creativity, and innovation (Kivunja 2015). Employers in a changing labor market increasingly seek employees who can easily adapt, apply, and transfer their skills and knowledge to new contexts (OECD 2018, 5). International alumni can be advisers to program directors in developing new curricula as well as serving as guest lecturers. Many academic programs engage local alumni in industry to advise on the current skills needed in the labor market. With the increase in tuition fees, potential for extensive debt after graduation, and high youth unemployment (Grzegorczyk and Wolff 2020; United Nations Development Programme 2020), many students and their families are now choosing universities that offer greater job opportunities after graduation. Given the increasing use of remote communication, virtual conferencing has become common practice. This shift allows universities to engage international alumni who can offer different perspectives from abroad to enrich the curriculum.

In the first example, the Royal Melbourne Institute of Technology University's international alumni share their experiences to help students develop twenty-first-century skills.

CASE STUDY

The Global Leadership Forum: Royal Melbourne Institute of Technology University
By Andy Coxall, MA

Institution	Royal Melbourne Institute of Technology University
Motto	Ready for life and work
Founded	1887
Location	Melbourne, Australia
Number of Students in 2020	97,193 (23% international onshore students, 18% international offshore students)
Number of Alumni in 2020	450,000 alumni in 130 countries
Department Responsible for International Alumni Relations	Alumni and Giving Team
Alumni Relations Office Website	https://www.rmit.edu.au/alumni-and-giving

In partnership with Common Purpose, a global not-for-profit organization that develops leaders who can work together across boundaries, the Royal Melbourne Institute of Technology University (RMIT) engaged their international alumni in helping students cultivate leadership skills. In 2019 in Melbourne, Australia, Common Purpose ran its flagship program with RMIT, the Global Leadership Forum, titled "Disruptor or Innovator, Campaigner or Catalyst, Revolution or Evolution. How Will You Change the World?" for 700 students. The 35 sessions and 39 speakers (the majority of whom were RMIT alumni chosen for their leadership and career experience and contacted by the RMIT alumni and giving team) reflected the many industries in which RMIT alumni go on to lead. Alumni included a senior leader of a global bank, a CEO at a nongovernmental organization tackling food poverty, social campaigners, and entrepreneurs. The platform provided international alumni with the chance to inspire students into action on the issues that matter to them: "Resilience and Mental Health"; "Here, Queer, and Held to Account: Being an Advocate for Transgender and Gender Diverse People"; and "Social Enterprises: A Positive Disruption to Homelessness

Support Services." At the end of the program, students completed a skills and competency assessment. The survey results indicated the following:
- 91 percent of students gained a better understanding of what it means to be a leader.
- 91 percent of students gained a better understanding of how leaders tackle key challenges.

More than 60 percent of the attendees then went on to earn a Developing Global Leadership microcredential, designed to help them deepen their knowledge and articulate what they learned. The microcredential is recorded on their academic transcripts and can be listed on their LinkedIn profiles.

This high-touch experience also offered international alumni purposeful ways to have a genuine impact on students, work on the issues that they are passionate about, and support and give back to the next generation of alumni. An alum of the MBA program at RMIT said, "I really enjoyed speaking with the students. They were so engaged and enthusiastic. One of our key focuses is on developing the next generation of leaders and changemakers, and programs like this are invaluable."

Student-alumni engagement has a real impact not only on students but also on international alumni, helping them reflect on themselves as leaders, their journey, and the impact they strive to achieve. Another alum, who has participated in the program four times, said, "I really loved the level of engagement and questions from the students in my master class, and I've now been inspired to write a collection of tricks and strategies that I've learned over the years that would help guide a future leader."

Alongside programs that allow international alumni to support students' learning and development in person, Common Purpose and RMIT have also developed many opportunities for international alumni to give back via online platforms, thus enabling alumni across the world to support RMIT's students in Asia and Australia. At the beginning of 2020, more than 250 students attended an online session with an RMIT alum based in London who is vice president of one of the world's leading financial service companies. After the session, a student said:

> My favorite key takeaway points from the session were the ideas of continuous learning and transferable skills, not underestimating the power (and correlation to success) of big data, and the most important thing is to be self-motivated in your career. I feel inspired and reassured I'm on the path to building the skills needed for the emerging workforce of the future.

International Internships and Jobs

According to a 2013 European Commission report, *Work-Based Learning in Europe: Practices and Policy Pointers*, a lack of workplace experience contributes to the growing skills gap and high youth unemployment rates. An extensive UK Commission for Employment and Skills survey (2016, 141) among 91,000 employers highlights not only the challenges of upgrading skills to work with technology but also the ongoing need for soft, people, and personal skills—in particular time management and task prioritization skills across all occupations. Higher education policymakers maintain that part of the solution lies in providing real-life work experience where students can apply academic and technical knowledge to develop employability skills, suggesting that work experience during higher education is helpful in securing employment upon graduation (O'Higgins and Pinedo 2018). Other scholars have found that only field-related and voluntary work experience has positive effects on labor market integration (Weiss, Klein, and Grauenhorst 2014). Furthermore, the findings indicate that international education is particularly valued when employers need graduates with good foreign language and decision-making skills. A comparative analysis of 31 countries confirms that employers place a higher value on international internships. The analysis revealed that overall, one in four employers value work placements abroad, compared to one in five employers valuing study abroad. In countries such as Cyprus, Greece, Italy, Latvia, Luxembourg, Portugal, and Turkey, international internships are rated as an important selection criterion by more than 40 percent of the surveyed companies (Van Mol 2017).

International alumni play an important role in providing internships abroad or connecting their alma mater with companies that do. In Istanbul, Turkey, Sabancı University (SU) has a Career Development and Alumni Relations (CDAR) Office that focuses its activities on two target groups—students and alumni—and, whenever possible, establishes strategic partnerships between both. Embracing the principle "once a student, then an alumnus, always one of us," SU engages its international alumni to better prepare students for the job market and equip them with contemporary skills and competencies, which help them secure internships and jobs abroad, particularly in the competitive technology industry of Silicon Valley.

CASE STUDY

Preparing Students for the Tech Industry: Sabancı University
By Şule Yalçın, MSc

Institution	Sabancı University
Motto	Creating and developing together
Founded	1996
Location	Istanbul, Turkey
Number of Students in 2020	5,421 (11% of which are international)
Number of Alumni in 2020	13,758 (5% of which are international)
Department Responsible for International Alumni Relations	Career Development and Alumni Relations Office
Alumni Relations Office Website	https://www.sabanciuniv.edu/en/alumni

Professional Development

To promote students' professional development before they graduate, the Career Development and Alumni Relations (CDAR) Office at Sabancı University (SU) runs various activities, such as career talks and simulation job interviews with alumni who work as human resources (HR) professionals. Other offerings include mentorship and employment through alumni and the virtual internships program.

International Career Talks with Alumni Who Work Abroad

The CDAR Office invites alumni to campus or hosts them online to provide students and recent graduates with the chance to learn about job opportunities and career paths outside of Turkey.

Simulation Job Interviews with Alumni in HR

The CDAR Office acts as a facilitator and brings students and alumni who work as HR professionals together through online or face-to-face job interview simulations. These simulations and the feedback provided by alumni better prepare students for real interviews.

International Alumni as Mentors and Employers

In this new cooperation, alumni who work abroad and want to recruit interns from Turkey contact the CDAR Office and share internship and job descriptions. Through its placement system, the CDAR Office disseminates information and coordinates selections. A panel composed of faculty specialized in the respective field selects applicants. In other words, the CDAR Office recruits on behalf of the alumni abroad, enhancing person-job fit and person-organization fit. Thus, through this cooperation, alumni benefit from the expertise and know-how of the CDAR Office, while SU students find the opportunity to work abroad. Moreover, through the European Commission's Erasmus+ Traineeship Program, the CDAR Office provides grants for some of the international internships, and the availability of such a grant has encouraged more alumni to get involved in this program.

Virtual Internship Programs

Given that alumni are familiar with the quality of education and professional training at SU, whenever possible alumni abroad appreciate working with their schoolmates and current SU students. The virtual internship program first started when an alum, who lives in the United Kingdom and works as a consultant on EU projects, requested to recruit two interns from the Faculty of Arts and Social Sciences to remotely work with her on a project. Now, the CDAR Office runs a considerable number of virtual internship programs in which SU alumni remotely mentor and employ students.

Revisiting Curriculum: Pathway to Silicon Valley Program

Selim Önal, an SU alum in engineering with a master's degree from the United States, works in Silicon Valley. Reflecting on the job hunting processes in Turkey and the United States and the reasons for low employability of Turkish engineers in Silicon Valley, he discussed the mismatch between the Turkish and international curricula with the director of the CDAR Office and the dean of engineering. Through a collaborative effort, the Faculty of Engineering and Natural Sciences (FENS) revised its curricula and the office started a new online interview simulation program to better prepare SU students for internship and job interviews with companies in Silicon Valley.

In 2017, the CDAR Office, with Önal's support, met the head of Turkish recruitment for Palantir Technologies, a prominent start-up in Silicon Valley. After this meeting, the CDAR Office initiated the Pathway to Silicon Valley program. This program aims to increase the number of SU students successfully completing interviews and earning internship or job offers from leading companies in the technology sector. The deans of FENS and the CDAR Office provided financial and HR support for the program; therefore, a syllabus and training schedule were developed for this program and for SU alike. The first year, 2017–18, was planned as the pilot implementation. Önal trained and mentored Betül Günay, an SU alum and teaching assistant at FENS, to run technical role-play interviews for 2 hours every week. Students were assigned coding challenges as homework, and under the supervision of Günay, they practiced interviews with each other. The program also included lectures and sessions run by other SU alumni. These alumni not only shared their experiences and conducted mock interviews but also contributed to students' placements by helping them with their applications, acting as mediators between students and companies, and providing recommendations. The pilot program received positive feedback from all participants. That year, one student was hired by Google. In light of the feedback, the program was revamped the following year, and instead of a teaching assistant, engineers from companies in Silicon Valley began running the training sessions.

Expanding Turkish Students' Reach in Silicon Valley

In 2019, the program was renamed DevPaths, and it has become a joint project between the CDAR Office and Crossing Paths, a not-for-profit organization based in California (see www.kesisenyollar.org/). Led by Önal, Crossing Paths provides Turkish youth with career coaching and mentoring.

DevPaths now covers both internship and full-time job opportunities, including a 15-week training module that is open to students from all Turkish universities. The training module simulates every stage of the hiring process in technology companies: résumé screening, behavioral interviews, technical phone screens, on-site interviews, and the hiring committee meetings. The CDAR Office helps by recruiting SU alumni engineers for the mock interview sessions, whereas Crossing Paths carries out the training sessions and mock interviews. During the sessions and interviews, alumni engineers analyze students' performances. The module ends with students' self-reflections and feedback from alumni and other engineers. The CDAR Office then builds a bridge between students, alumni, and companies. It also undertakes the referral process by bringing students who completed the program with the highest performance together with distinguished alumni and other engineers working in companies in Silicon Valley. Alumni and other engineers then help the students find jobs by providing recommendations. Given the high number of applications that Silicon Valley companies receive, internal references for students greatly increase their chances of being considered for a job.

Sabancı Informatics Days: A One-Day Career Event

DevPaths's success has paved the way for Sabancı Informatics Days, a one-day career event originally held on campus in December 2019. This career event, specialized in technology, was the first of its kind in Turkey. It brought more than 40 engineers representing companies in Silicon Valley, professors, alumni, and other professionals in the technology sector together with more than 200 high school and university students. During the event, participants learned about the latest developments in technology, attended career talks, participated in mock interviews, and networked with each other and the speakers.

By summer 2020, about 100 students had participated in the program and completed job applications. The objective was to have at least 40 of them receive job offers from at least one of their top-three target companies. Over the first 2 years, 56 students were recommended by the alumni engaged in DevPaths, and 42 of them were offered a position either as an intern or full-time employee by Silicon Valley companies, including Amazon, Facebook, Microsoft, Palantir, and many others.

With this program, the CDAR Office intends to strengthen its relations not only with its alumni abroad but also with the technology companies, and to become one of the biggest talent pools of Silicon Valley in Europe, the Middle East, and Africa. Since the launch of DevPaths in 2019, 46 alumni have contributed to the program by either carrying out a session or conducting mock interviews. They have also acted as a bridge between their companies and participating students. In the years to come, the CDAR Office aims to get more international alumni on board and, whenever possible, integrate their feedback, expertise, and knowledge to continue SU's motto: "creating and developing together."

> **Voice from the Field: Selim Önal, MS, SU alum and founder of Crossing Paths**
>
> Having worked at Google and Palantir, I organized and attended more than 20 university events in China, Turkey, and the United States and knew that there was a huge demand for well-trained talent in the tech industry—but there was never enough supply. This gap motivated three of my friends and me to establish a not-for-profit organization to coach and mentor Turkish students who want to work in Silicon Valley. I knew that my alma mater, SU, had huge potential to be a pioneer in this field in Turkey. SU has always provided a sound professional foundation. However, over the years, I observed that the interviews carried out in Silicon Valley differ from traditional ones in other fields and regions; hence, students needed special preparation. When I shared this observation with Şule Yalçın, manager of the CDAR Office, in early 2017, she took immediate action and mobilized all relevant stakeholders. I also came together with the dean of the Faculty of Engineering and Natural Sciences and various faculty members from the Department of Computer Science and Engineering. They started offering an alternative curriculum path tailored for students targeting Silicon Valley companies and added an introductory computer science course to the curriculum. More than 10 years ago, when I was still a student at SU, the motto "creating and developing together" was everywhere. Over the years, I have experienced that with graduation, this togetherness does not come to an end. Alumni are always included, despite their place of residence.

Mentoring

Mentoring can be defined as an exchange of knowledge and experience between mentor and mentee. Internationally, mentoring is primarily used in professional education and training or to help new employees in their introduction to their job (Arnesson and Albinsson 2017). Mentoring benefits both mentor and mentee. Students learn knowledge and skills, as well as professional socialization and personal development that can facilitate success in college and beyond. International alumni mentors can contribute their know-how of finding jobs abroad and navigating a new career in a foreign country or back home. Alumni mentors also benefit from mentoring programs when they share their expertise, experience, and skills while coaching. They learn from mentees' new perspectives, which may spark self-reflection. Also, they can use their creativity to address challenges expressed by their mentees. But above all, many alumni mentors experience personal satisfaction in helping students bridge their studies with the labor market or aiding fellow alumni in growing within their professional sector. Figure 1 summarizes some benefits of mentoring programs described by the Institute for Corporate Responsibility and Sustainability (n.d.). These benefits can be emphasized when recruiting alumni mentors and promoting the program among students.

Figure 1. Benefits of Mentorship

What are the benefits for mentees?	What are the benefits for mentors?
1. Improving self-confidence and self-esteem	1. Enhancing coaching and listening skills
2. Broadening horizons and accessing new experiences	2. Developing and practicing a personal style of leadership
3. Recognizing achievements and raising aspirations	3. Learning new perspectives and approaches
4. Motivating self-directed learning	4. Giving back to one's industry
5. Improving performance and use of talents and expertise	5. Gaining recognition and respect
6. Increasing job satisfaction	6. Achieving personal satisfaction
7. Networking	7. Exercising creativity
8. Gaining career opportunities and career mobility	8. Extending professional and personal networks
9. Giving and receiving feedback	9. Experiencing how to deal with challenging situations
10. Developing visibility within an organization	10. Demonstrating expertise and sharing knowledge and skills

In the Netherlands, Erasmus University's Rotterdam School of Management exemplifies how a school can revamp its mentoring program within a short period of time to engage a large number of alumni and provide career support for students.

Chapter 6

CASE STUDY

Enhancing MentorMe Effectiveness: Rotterdam School of Management, Erasmus University
By Juan Maldonado Alcazar, MBA

Institution	Rotterdam School of Management, Erasmus University
Motto	To be a force for positive change in the world
Founded	1970
Location	Rotterdam, the Netherlands
Number of Students in 2020	7,150 (approximately 30% of which are international)
Number of Alumni in 2020	45,000 (37% of which are international)
Department Responsible for International Alumni Relations	Corporate and Alumni Relations Office
Alumni Relations Office Website	https://www.rsm.nl/alumni/

The RSM MentorMe program at Erasmus University's Rotterdam School of Management (RSM) has become one of the most successful mentoring programs in the Netherlands and a model for universities internationally. RSM MentorMe was first launched in 2016, but within 2 years it had only attracted 530 alumni. By June 2018, it was revamped to enhance its success by further involving stakeholders: alumni and mentees provided feedback; the platform provider helped RSM staff implement design and usage changes; and academic directors made mentoring part of their programs. In 2 years, RSM MentorMe transformed into a pillar of alumni engagement, with more than 7,500 members worldwide logging more than a thousand mentoring sessions per year, and more than 1,000 alumni volunteering their time. Mentors have become engaged and provide recruitment opportunities, serve as guest speakers, and facilitate corporate relations, making them some of the institution's most valuable alumni volunteers.

Initial Challenges

To learn more about the program's initial challenges, 40 alumni worldwide were interviewed about their experience. RSM found the following weaknesses:
1. Students were ill-prepared for sessions with mentors and booked meetings just hours in advance, giving mentors no time to accommodate and prepare for them.
2. The default matching system was a problem; some mentors were overbooked, while others went without any student meetings.
3. There was no follow-up after the first meeting.
4. The university did not provide much volunteer recognition.

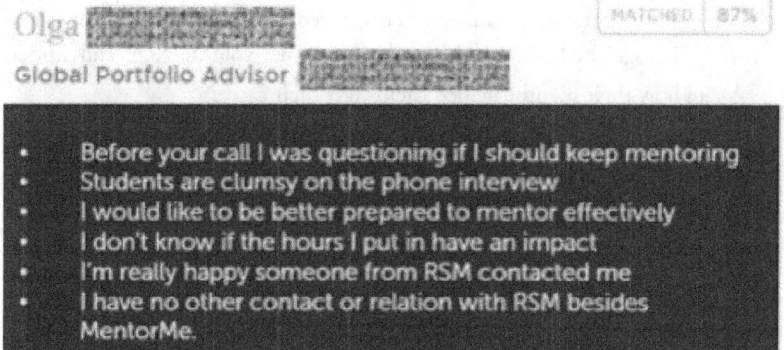

Source: Image courtesy of Juan Maldonado Alcazar.

Students' insights revealed that they did not feel supported before going into a session. Most students found the prospect of talking to a successful alumni daunting. Data showed that students who used the platform once were likely to engage in a second conversation and that young alumni also wanted access to mentors to jump-start their careers.

Data-Driven Improvements

The corporate and alumni relations department teamed up with most academic departments at RSM, and consequently, a student's first consultation in RSM MentorMe is now a graded assignment in the course "Your Future Career." With the career center, the alumni relations department created videos and tutorials to support first consultations with mentors in the platform. MentorMe serves more than 1,210 students annually, and after their first session, more than 60 percent of the students engage in new consultations with mentors without any additional incentive from RSM. Other improvements in the program after feedback include the following:

1. The default availability was changed to times when mentors are out of office (after 7:00 p.m.) without impacting their weekends.
2. Students and young alumni were required to book a consultation at least 3 days in advance so mentors could better plan their time.
3. Students were provided with live networking workshops and templates for starting conversations to prepare them with relevant questions for their mentors.
4. MentorMe Season was instituted, starting every September. This promotion tripled the amount of requested consultations.
5. An alumni recognition dinner was organized. The top-rated mentor receives the Distinguished Alumni Award for his or her volunteering, and students share how their mentor helped them start their careers.

In 2 years, 4,000 mentoring sessions have been scheduled through MentorMe. This mentoring program shows how involving a community of international alumni, students, faculty, staff, and companies can yield powerful results while increasing alumni pride and strengthening their relationships with their alma mater. In fact, MentorMe received the silver CASE Circle of Excellence Award in 2020.

Lifelong Learning

In 1929, Basil Alfred Yeaxlee wrote the first book on lifelong learning, titled *Lifelong Education: A Sketch of the Range and Significance of the Adult Education Movement*. Almost a century later, as technology makes old job skills superfluous and economic changes bring new business models, employers and society as a whole rely on higher education institutions to train and retrain talent. As stated in the *OECD Skills Strategy 2019* report:

> The traditional approach of front-end loading skills development is increasingly untenable in a world of rapid technological, economic and societal changes. Learning over the life course is not only for the highly skilled; it is essential for all citizens, in order to become full and active participants in the economy and society. (OECD 2019, 74)

Some scholars propose higher education as a life journey that runs parallel to alumni's entire careers: "Rather than viewing higher education as a discrete event that occurs between the ages of 18 and 24 and prepares students for their entire working lives, a long-term view is needed in which an educational journey runs parallel to a career" (Auguste and Chopra 2018, 4). Lifelong learning, essential for sustaining the success and growth of students and alumni, provides higher education institutions with an impetus to engage international alumni throughout their lifetime.

As knowledge creators, many universities already offer their alumni lifelong learning opportunities through in-person and online experiences. For example, INSEAD Business School in Fontainebleau, France, has a designated section on lifelong learning on its alumni association's web page (https://www.insead.edu/alumni/lifelong-learning), which includes a series of webinars on exigent topics, such as gender, racism, and work-life design. In the United States, the University of Chicago's lifelong learning program offers different options through its alumni website, including lectures on iTunes, courses, and educational YouTube videos. Tecnológico de Monterrey in Mexico teamed up with two other universities in Latin America, Pontificia Universidad Católica de Chile and Universidad de los Andes in Colombia, to offer its international alumni courses and certificates through Coursera. Universidad ESAN, as described in the following case study, contributes to its alumni's lifelong learning through postgraduate study abroad opportunities.

CASE STUDY

Alumni Study Abroad Programs: Universidad ESAN
By Mariella Olivos, PhD

Institution	Universidad ESAN
Mission	To offer education that contributes to the development of leaders and responsible professionals capable of responding to the demands of the globalized climate and participating actively in the creation of an equal and fair society.
Founded	1963 as a business school and 2008 as a university
Location	Lima, Peru

Number of Students in 2020	8,500 students (6% of which are international)
Number of Alumni in 2020	14,000 (11% of which are international)
Department Responsible for International Alumni Relations	Individual staff members
Websites	• Bachelor-level blog: https://chapteralumniesan.blogspot.com/ • Graduate-level website: https://esanalumni.esan.edu.pe/

One of international higher education's main objectives is to teach intercultural competencies to students. International education spurs intercultural competence through study abroad programs, multicultural classrooms, and internationalized curricula. For the majority of students, studying abroad is not feasible due to economic barriers or because they must complete their academic workload at a certain time. But what happens when these students without a study abroad experience transition to alumni and get jobs? Do they still want to participate in study abroad programs?

In Peru, Universidad ESAN has opened opportunities for its recent graduates to study abroad. Study abroad is offered in the bachelor's programs, but most of ESAN's undergraduate students cannot participate due to financial barriers. Mariella Olivos, ESAN's associate director of undergraduate programs and head of the international office, realized that once recent graduates earned jobs, they wanted to participate in short study abroad programs.

ESAN annually receives around 150 incoming international students, but it only sends a maximum of 50 students abroad. To solve this imbalance, Olivos saw an opportunity by establishing agreements with several partner universities to accept ESAN's recent graduates in their summer or winter programs as part of the ESAN Alumni Study Abroad Program. The programs usually include visits to organizations and companies in the public and private sectors. Upon their return, alumni write about their experiences in a blog post for the ESAN alumni website, where the program is further promoted. Similar to other institutional exchange programs, this one does not exchange tuition fees. The ESAN Alumni Study Abroad Program only registers alumni who have graduated in the past 2 years and are between 24 and 27 years old. Olivos says:

Once recent graduates have a job, they are able to pay their own traveling and living expenses abroad. We make sure that the courses available are short since [the alumni] will need to take a short leave from their jobs to attend a three- or eight-week course. We make courses available to them free of tuition fees....In this way, ESAN University can still be relevant to fulfill a dream most of them have had during their studies.

Jacqueline Dextre, an ESAN alum, participated in a three-week program on international finance at Aalto University in Espoo, Finland. Apart from the academic knowledge, Dextre believes one of greatest assets she gained from the study abroad program is the international network she built with other participants.

Conclusion

Employability for the twenty-first century needs to be an integral part of higher education given the continually evolving labor market. Many universities are turning to their international alumni to help prepare students for future jobs abroad. International alumni can function as advisers, mentors, and employers because they know the level of education offered by their alma mater. Universities now also recognize the importance of offering lifelong learning to meet the demands of a dynamic labor market, and thus can accompany international alumni along their career paths. Opening opportunities to students through internships or jobs and offering lifelong learning to alumni builds a two-way relationship. In a global economy, universities that can nurture an international alumni network with a culture of giving and lifelong learning will be able to count on their alumni's support to help solve problems in today's professional and economic sectors.

References

Arnesson, Kerstin, and Gunilla Albinsson. 2017. "Mentorship—A Pedagogical Method for Integration of Theory and Practice in Higher Education." *Nordic Journal of Studies in Educational Policy* 3, 3:202–17.

Auguste, Byron, and Karan Chopra. 2018. "Lifelong Learning: Higher Education for a World of Speed and Scale." *International Educator*, May/June. https://www.nafsa.org/ie-magazine/issue/27/3/may-june-2018.

Council for Advancement and Support of Education (CASE). 2020. "From Zero to Hero: The Journey of RSM MentorMe." Circle of Excellence Awards. https://www.case.org/awards/circle-excellence/2020/zero-hero-journey-rsm-mentorme.

Dextre, Jacqueline. 2017. "Summer Program Experience at Aalto University—Finland." *Chapter Alumni Esan* (blog). August 11. https://chapteralumniesan.blogspot.com/2017/08/experiencia-summer-program-en-aalto.html.

European Commission. 2013. *Work-Based Learning in Europe: Practices and Policy Pointers.* https://www.skillsforemployment.org/KSP/en/Details/?dn=WCMSTEST4_057845.

Grzegorczyk, Monika, and Guntram B. Wolff. 2020. "The Scarring Effect of COVID-19: Youth Unemployment in Europe." *Bruegel.* November 28. https://www.bruegel.org/2020/11/the-scarring-effect-of-covid-19-youth-unemployment-in-europe/.

Harari, Yuval Noah. 2019. *21 Lessons for the 21st Century.* London: Jonathan Cape.

Institute for Corporate Responsibility and Sustainability (ICRS). n.d. "Guidelines for Mentors and Mentees." https://icrs.info/cpd/mentoring/guidelines#What%20makes%20a%20successful%20mentoring%20relationship?.

Kivunja, Charles. 2015. "Teaching Students to Learn and to Work Well with 21st Century Skills: Unpacking the Career and Life Skills Domain of the New Learning Paradigm." *International Journal of Higher Education* 4, 1.

O'Higgins, Niall, and Luis Pinedo. 2018. *Interns and Outcomes: Just How Effective Are Internships as a Bridge to Stable Employment?* EMPLOYMENT Working Paper No. 241. Geneva, Switzerland: International Labour Organization.

Organisation for Economic Co-operation and Development (OECD). 2018. *Preparing Our Youth for an Inclusive and Sustainable World: The OECD PISA Global Competence Framework.* Paris, France: OECD. https://www.oecd.org/education/Global-competency-for-an-inclusive-world.pdf.

Organisation for Economic Co-operation and Development (OECD). 2019. *OECD Skills Strategy 2019: Skills to Shape a Better Future.* Paris, France: OECD. https://www.oecd.org/skills/oecd-skills-strategy-2019-9789264313835-en.htm.

UK Commission for Employment and Skills. 2016. *Employer Skills Survey 2015: UK Results.* London, UK: UK Commission for Employment and Skills.

https://assets.publishing.service.gov.uk/government/uploads/system/uploads/attachment_data/file/704104/Employer_Skills_Survey_2015_UK_Results-Amended-2018.pdf.

United Nations Development Programme. 2020. *Human Development Report 2020*. New York, NY: United Nations Development Programme. http://hdr.undp.org/sites/default/files/hdr2020.pdf.

Van Mol, Christof. 2017. "Do Employers Value International Study and Internships? A Comparative Analysis of 31 Countries." *Geoforum* 78:52–60.

Weiss, Felix, Markus Klein, and Thomas Grauenhorst. 2014. "The Effects of Work Experience During Higher Education on Labour Market Entry: Learning by Doing or an Entry Ticket?" *Work Employment & Society* 28, 5:788–807.

World Economic Forum (WEF). 2018. *The Future of Jobs Report 2018*. Geneva, Switzerland: World Economic Forum. https://www.weforum.org/reports/the-future-of-jobs-report-2018.

Yeaxlee, Basil A. 1929. *Lifelong Education: A Sketch of the Range and Significance of the Adult Education Movement*. London, UK: Cassell.

Chapter 6

Innovation and Social Responsibility

Advancements of the Fourth Industrial Revolution (see page 135) promote innovation for economic growth and social development. Innovation, "an idea, practice, or object that is perceived as new by an individual or other unit of adoption" (Rogers 2003, 189), is no longer exclusive to the science and technology sectors; it now takes place in all parts of the economy, society, and politics (Schwab 2015). *The Oslo Manual*, used to collect and measure innovation data, further defines innovation as "the implementation of a new or significantly improved product (good or service), or process, a new marketing method, or a new organizational method in business practices, workplace organisation or external relations" (OECD 2005, 46). Despite the myriad definitions provided by scholars and governmental organizations, many share three common elements: newness, improvement, and diffusion (Edison, bin Ali, and Torkar 2013). As part of the innovation topology, social innovation is defined as new ideas that meet social needs, create social relationships, and form new collaborations (Howaldt and Schwarz 2010). In recent years, the need for creative solutions in stimulating sustainable growth has drawn more attention to social innovation (Urama and Acheampong 2013). Universities, governments, industries, and civil societies are increasingly investing in social innovation labs that support start-ups, incubators, accelerators, and other movements to bridge knowledge gaps (Kreutz 2016). Innovative economies are more productive, resilient, and adaptable to change, and can offer better standards of living (OECD 2015). "Strengthening innovation is therefore a fundamental challenge for countries in their quest for greater prosperity and better lives" (OECD 2015, 3).

Since 2007, the Global Innovation Index (GII) has ranked world economies according to their innovation capabilities. In 2020, Switzerland ranked as the world leader in innovation for the tenth consecutive year (GII 2020). So what makes Switzerland a world leader in innovation? Three factors stand out: (1) investment in human capital and research; (2) strong collaboration between the corporate sector and universities; and (3) triangular cooperation with start-ups, larger companies, and academic research labs. These factors foster innovation and collaborations to meet social needs, such as supporting start-ups, creating new jobs by investing in human capital, and solving problems through applied research. All of the top 10 countries ranked in the GII 2020 invest in research and development and have strong universities with established networks in both the public and private sectors (Dutta, Lanvin, and Wunsch-Vincent 2020).

Human talent, innovation's cornerstone, depends on the education and training to develop skills (e.g., entrepreneurial, technological, and social), identify business opportunities, generate ideas, learn when to take risks, and network. According to the European University Association (2018), all of these skills are indispensable to innovative cities, regions, and countries; therefore, universities have an essential role in developing, attracting, and retaining human talent in their innovation ecosystems.

Universities should include international alumni networks in their innovation ecosystems because, through their knowledge, contacts, and entrepreneurial mindsets, alumni can serve as social innovators. This section presents various ways in which universities, alumni associations, and organizations engage international alumni as social innovators in creating triangular collaborations with start-ups, larger companies, and academic researchers. It includes three examples from the field: (1) NL alumni network-Netherlands, an international alumni association that supports those entering the Dutch labor market, seeking career and personal development, and pursuing entrepreneurship opportunities; (2) the citywide Barcelona Science and Technology Diplomacy Hub, which creates ample opportunities to connect international alumni with their alma maters, scientists, researchers, and innovators; and (3) the University of Manchester and its award-winning Day of Action, which embraces the Sustainable Development Goals (SDGs) around the world. These programs inspire and empower international alumni communities to act as socially responsible global citizens.

Entrepreneurship in Higher Education

Entrepreneurship, a critical component of innovation, creates jobs, drives progress, and contributes to economic growth. Many governments and policymakers, therefore, aim to increase the number of entrepreneurs in their country and aid their development (WEF 2015). An OECD paper, *Entrepreneurship in Education*, argues that infusing entrepreneurship into curricula can increase students' motivation, engagement, and deep learning because students can experience creating value for others with what they have learned (Lackéus 2015). Given the urgency of finding solutions for sustainable development, the nexus of innovation and entrepreneurship has become essential for higher education (Kardos 2012). Thus, teaching entrepreneurship provides myriad positive effects in economic growth, job creation, and increased societal resilience, as well as individual growth, increased academic engagement, and improved equality. The World Economic Forum's 2019 report *How to Build an Entrepreneurial University* introduces a useful framework to guide higher education institutions and emphasizes the importance of strong partnerships with industry:

> Relationships require a foundation of trust and an understanding of the interests of each party—and nurturing these relationships throughout the partnership is equally critical. As leadership change takes place at different rates in academia, start-ups and large corporations, it can be challenging to re-establish trust and re-align on the goals in the face of change. It's important to have a strategic consensus to sustain the essence of mutual goals and reinforce the relationship to maintain a solid relationship throughout their partnerships. (Eisenberg, Gann, and Yoon 2019, 4)

Given higher education's role in producing innovation, international alumni can be strategic partners as entrepreneurs and visionaries. They can help build trust, contribute know-how, and sustain mutual goals in the triangular cooperation among their alma mater, industry, and governmental sector. International alumni networks, higher education institutions, and other stakeholders can collaborate in multidisciplinary networks to stimulate entrepreneurship, retain talent, and encourage sustainable development.

As a social innovator, the NL alumni network-Netherlands is a nationwide alumni network that meets the needs of international students and recent international graduates wishing to live and work in the Netherlands. The NL alumni network-Netherlands supports Dutch universities and the government in retaining international talent through a community of international alumni volunteers who help others navigate the labor market and provide community.

CASE STUDY

International Alumni Entrepreneurs Connecting Education, Innovation, and Trade: NL alumni network-Netherlands
By Sandra Rincón, MSc

Association	NL alumni network-Netherlands
Motto	Here2Contribute
Founded	2017
Location	The Netherlands
Number of Students in 2020	2,200 (100% of which are international)
Number of Alumni in 2020	1,500 (100% of which are international)
Divisions Responsible for International Alumni Relations	President and board members of the association
Websites and Social Media	• https://www.nlalumni.nl/group/alumni-in-the-netherlands/134/ • http://here2work.nl/ • https://www.here2start.nl/ • https://www.youtube.com/channel/UC797JpD66GxgF7_ODLAqWTQ

Ranked sixth in the 2020 GII, the Netherlands engages alumni worldwide to support its top innovation sectors as well as attract and retain international talent. In 2017, the Dutch Advisory Council for Science, Technology and Innovation (AWTI) presented the *STI Diplomacy* report to the Dutch government. The report proposed a proactive national strategy to internationalize science, technology, and innovation by (1) extending the diplomatic networks of science, technology, and innovation; (2) attracting and retaining international talent; (3) strengthening and expanding international collaboration; and (4) branding the Netherlands as a country with strengths in knowledge production and innovation (AWTI 2017).

Nuffic, the Dutch organization for international education, responded to these requests by articulating a national alumni strategy that comprises four pillars: (1) trade promotion; (2) knowledge exchange and innovation; (3) education promotion and connections with talent; and (4) public diplomacy and local knowledge. Each pillar engages international alumni as key actors in connecting education, innovation, and trade (Nuffic 2018). In 2009, Nuffic established the Holland Alumni network, which it rebranded as NL alumni network in 2021. To date, the network has grown to more than 70,000 international alumni and 80 online alumni associations worldwide. All alumni and communities register in an online platform funded and managed by Nuffic. The online platform allows universities and alumni associations to create their own communities, connect directly to their international alumni, and promote their events. As a result of governmental policy changes and budget constraints, Nuffic refocused its alumni strategy to support the country's top innovation sectors (see www.topsectoren.nl/innovatie) and anchors its activities in four thematic alumni communities: (1) food and nutrition security; (2) water, energy, and climate; (3) security and the rule of law; and (4) sexual and reproductive health and rights. These themes strengthen the top innovation sectors and the Orange Knowledge Programme, which grants scholarships to mid-career professionals contributing to sustainability. Many of the active alumni registered in the platform have received scholarships to participate in the Orange Knowledge Programme. Nuffic's alumni strategy is a concrete example of how to embrace international alumni engagement to advance innovation and sustainable development.

NL alumni network-Netherlands

To support the Netherlands's national alumni strategy in retaining international talent, Nuffic provided seed funding to establish the NL alumni network-Netherlands. Launched in 2017 as the only nationwide association for international students and alumni living in the Netherlands, the association has grown in 3 years to more than 3,700 members, representing all Dutch higher education institutions. Completely managed by international alumni volunteers, NL alumni network-Netherlands functions as a social innovator by implementing new services to meet the international students and alumni residing in the Netherlands. Furthermore, NL alumni network-Netherlands has developed two initiatives—Here2Work and

Here2Start—that aim to meet the needs of international talent and entrepreneurs by making them feel welcome and helping them create social relationships, open job opportunities, and build new collaborations to start businesses in the Netherlands.

Here2Work

Many international students take advantage of the orientation year provided by the Dutch government to extend residency for a year while looking for jobs in the Netherlands. Recent international graduates often have difficulty understanding what they need to do to extend their residency and how they should go about looking for a job or internship. They often lack a network of peers who work in Dutch companies that hire internationals. Many of the national or local job fairs do not offer vacancies for internationals, nor do they cater to an international audience. When international alumni move from one city to another within the Netherlands, they often feel that they are starting all over again. The NL alumni network-Netherlands alleviates some of the obstacles by offering frequent in-person and online events through its regional communities. These events aim to help members navigate the Dutch job market and, more important, build friendships with other international and Dutch alumni.

To celebrate International Student Week 2020, the association launched Here2Work as the first nationwide virtual job fair available exclusively to international students and alumni who want to work in the Netherlands. It welcomed more than 700 participants, and 50 international alumni donated their time and expertise.

Here2Start

In 2019, the NL alumni network-Netherlands launched another initiative, the Here2Start Fest, as the first nationwide event exclusively for international students and alumni looking to start a business in the Netherlands, thereby promoting innovation in the country. It attracted more than 150 participants to Amsterdam, and 20 international alumni volunteers helped organize it and line up more than 30 speakers, who shared their own stories of building start-ups. In July 2020, Here2Start held its second event online during two half days. It welcomed 300 participants and 40 speakers and facilitated speed business networking and one-on-one mentoring sessions. The 2020 theme was "Creating Bridges Between the Netherlands and Colombia," and sessions were held in English and Spanish to attract participants from both countries. Here2Start has grown to become more than a platform; it is now a community of more than 300 international alumni entrepreneurs committed to helping international students and other international alumni start and grow their business in the Netherlands. To build bridges between the Netherlands and other countries, Here2Start will select a different country each year, invite its representatives to the program, and further facilitate business landing opportunities. Both events in 2019 and 2020 were cofinanced by NL alumni network-Netherlands and two other international alumni members.

> **Voice from the Field: María Lucía Bermúdez, MSc, cofounder of Here2Start and Tilburg University alum**
> Our main goal with Here2Start is to promote entrepreneurship to the international students and alumni community in the Netherlands so they can see there are other ways to a career path. I see that international alumni bring innovative concepts and networks to the start-up ecosystem. I had my own business in my country, Colombia, before coming to the Netherlands. When I moved to Amsterdam, it was tough to get a visa to start my business. I struggled a lot because the system was not inclusive of international entrepreneurs. That is why I want to help other international students and alumni avoid all the challenges I had. Since I moved to Amsterdam, I have been creating bridges between the Netherlands and Colombia. In the online Here2Start Fest, we showcased Colombia, and the positive reactions from entrepreneurs on both sides of the ocean were amazing. I have been approached by both alma maters in the Netherlands and Colombia, as well as governmental organizations, to speak on international entrepreneurship. Countries in Latin America are looking for ways to internationalize not only their universities, but their innovation ecosystem. We also want to make Here2Start a platform to increase and measure the impact of international business owners in Dutch start-up ecosystems and provide consultancy to universities and governments on what it takes to attract international entrepreneurs.

NL alumni network-Netherlands works closely with universities, governmental organizations, expat centers, and industry in supporting collaboration, knowledge exchange, entrepreneurship, innovation, and inclusion. While many universities around the world do not have access to a national alumni strategy nor a global alumni network subsidized by the government, there are various takeaways that can be learned from the Dutch initiative. First, international alumni can be key actors in advancing not only university-level but also national strategies, giving universities leverage in demonstrating that international alumni have meaningful roles in pursuing service missions and contributing to society. Second, international alumni networks can further strengthen the university's collaboration with the government and industry, since trade and innovation are also closely linked with multidisciplinary networks. Third, an international alumni network can help retain talent by sharing common experiences on living in-country as immigrants and how to navigate the local labor market. Last, an international alumni network can stimulate innovation by opening networks to the start-up ecosystem.

Science Diplomacy

In today's world, climate change, food security, migration, epidemics, refugees and migration, poverty reduction, and water security know no boundaries. Knowledge diplomacy is defined as "the role of international higher education, research, and innovation in building/strengthening relations between and among countries" (Knight 2018, 8). Knowledge diplomacy, according to Knight (2018, 8), "can (and should) be understood as a two-way reciprocal process whereby relations between and among countries can enhance international higher education and research." Knight further distinguishes education, science, cultural, public, and issue-related diplomacy as narrower in scope and with specific outcomes.

Science diplomacy, although not new, is now more important than ever given the scientific dimension of the current global challenges. "An important role for science diplomacy is to build bridges between science, technology and innovation practices, national interests, as well as global challenges" (Gabriel 2020). Science diplomacy provides scientific advice to support foreign policy, international scientific cooperation, and international relations. Moreover, science diplomacy can deliver research results to solve global challenges through evidence-based policymaking. Activities and research around the topic of science diplomacy have increased since the seminal 2010 Royal Society report titled *New Frontiers in Science Diplomacy*.

In Spain, the Barcelona Science and Technology Diplomacy Hub provides a unique example of how international alumni can bridge the triangular collaboration (between universities, industry, and government) to ignite science diplomacy and innovation.

Chapter 6

CASE STUDY

Internationalizing Innovation Through Citywide Alumni Networks: Barcelona Science and Technology Diplomacy Hub
By Alexis Roig, MSc

Organization	Barcelona Science and Technology Diplomacy Hub (SciTech DiploHub)
Motto	Connecting the dots in science, technology, higher education, and innovation between Barcelona and the world
Founded	2018
Location	Barcelona, Spain
Number of Alumni in 2020	More than 1,500
Department Responsible for International Alumni Relations	CEO
Website and Social Media	• http://www.scitechdiplohub.org/barcelona-alumni • https://twitter.com/SciTechDiploHub • https://www.linkedin.com/company/scitechdiplohub • https://www.instagram.com/scitechdiplohub • https://www.youtube.com/scitechdiplohub • https://www.flickr.com/scitechdiplohub

Barcelona Science and Technology Diplomacy Hub (SciTech DiploHub) is a nonprofit public-private partnership supported by Barcelona's leading research centers, universities, nonprofit organizations, start-ups, corporations, and public institutions. It aims to elevate the roles of science, technology, and cities in foreign policy and make Barcelona an influential player through its contribution to global challenges. Barcelona Alumni is a global network of high-achieving scientists, researchers, technology experts, and innovation leaders trained in Barcelona and based abroad. Led by SciTech DiploHub, Barcelona Alumni is a strategic pillar of Barcelona's science diplomacy strategy.

Objectives to Meet Challenges

Higher education and talent mobility play a decisive role in public diplomacy and global influence. International alumni are key allies and advocates of Barcelona's economic, social, and cultural value beyond its geographical areas. Given the escalating governmental budget cuts in education, many of Barcelona's higher education and research institutions cannot dedicate resources to develop their own international alumni networks. Consequently, Barcelona's knowledge ecosystem has the potential for more international visibility and greater numbers of international students, researchers, and engaged alumni. Thus, alumni have remained an untapped resource for Barcelona's science diplomacy strategy. Uncoordinated or overlapping policies at different levels of government were identified as a relevant challenge. Therefore, SciTech DiploHub's main objectives are to coordinate internationalization strategies, align interests and priorities, and achieve greater coherence with the government. SciTech DiploHub's Barcelona manifesto delineates its *raison d'être*, vision, and goals. SciTech DiploHub, launched in 2018, has both the financial support and active collaboration of Barcelona's higher education research institutions, government, businesses, scientists, and technology experts.

Building Barcelona's Internationalization

Barcelona alumni can be intercultural communicators; ambassadors of the city's innovation ecosystem; and promoters for education, business, and trade. They increase the international recognition and visibility of Barcelona's research, higher education, and innovation ecosystem. Thousands of alumni who have studied, done research, or worked in Barcelona are now building their professional careers in world-class universities, research centers, and cutting-edge tech companies around the world. Engaging Barcelona alumni contributes to Barcelona's internationalization and innovation strategies in several dimensions:

1. **Research and education:** The alumni network creates opportunities for academic, scientific, and business partnerships, thus adding value to the ecosystem's research institutions and innovation industries. It exerts a multiplier effect on the internationalization of Barcelona's innovation ecosystem. Alumni can promote Barcelona as a reliable partner in science and technology and as a destination for higher education and training.
2. **Business:** The network develops talent for industry, investment, and entrepreneurship, supporting the ecosystem's economic development.

Barcelona Alumni seeks to better understand international trends and strategic markets, allowing Barcelona's ecosystem to anticipate priorities, research needs, and public policies.

3. **Public diplomacy:** The alumni network conveys a commitment to global challenges, responsible research and innovation, and the United Nations SDGs. A considerable number of alumni hold influential and high-responsibility positions in their respective locations. Therefore, strengthening relationships with them promotes a better understanding of global challenges and strategic markets.

Barcelona Alumni's Needs and Opportunities

After holding an interactive design-thinking workshop with more than 100 alumni and almost 150 meetings in 12 cities around the globe, Barcelona alumni expressed the following needs and opportunities:

1. **Global community:** To be part of a global community to identify, connect, and network with fellow alumni around the world; to foster professional development through mentoring programs, job exchanges, and multiple institutional affiliations; and to hold in-person meetings and events to connect cities where alumni live and innovation hubs with Barcelona's universities, companies, and research institutions.
2. **Visibility and updates:** To highlight the value of positioning Barcelona's global talent community in the public sphere to raise awareness and strengthen the positive social and economic impact of science, technology, and innovation, and to receive tailored updates and information regarding Barcelona's knowledge ecosystem, including its higher education institutions, research centers, and technology companies.
3. **Global policy lab:** To leverage all alumni's experiences, ideas, and knowledge to influence specific programs at Barcelona's institutions and improve the design of evidence-based policies.

Results of Barcelona Alumni Project

One of the significant results of the Barcelona Alumni project has been to map out the community. With more than 1,000 members in more than 30 countries, the Barcelona Alumni Network has the largest number of members in the United States (more than 350), United Kingdom (more than 250), Germany (more than 150), and Switzerland (more than 80). Their main areas of expertise are life sciences (more than 350), information technologies and engineering (more than 300), fundamental sciences (more than 200), and social and economic sciences (more than 150). Many Barcelona alumni are senior research fellows or professors at leading research institutions and international universities. A significant number of Barcelona alumni lead technology start-ups, either as founders and chief executive officers, chief scientific officers, or chief technology officers, as well as work as product managers in scientific industries. Through various surveys, interviews, and social media campaigns, alumni have indicated where they live and work as well as their main interests in being part of the alumni community. This information has facilitated strategic decision-making to better invest resources.

In May 2019, the first regional chapter abroad was launched in Boston during Barcelona Innovation Day at Harvard University. The Barcelona Innovation Days are events held in cities where large numbers of Barcelona alumni live. These events bring together stakeholders from academia, start-ups, industry, and public institutions. Barcelona alumni showcase best practices in science and technology, engaging with fellow alumni in their fields and with Barcelona's business partners. Between 2018 and 2020, meetings with international alumni members were held in Amsterdam, Berlin, Boston, Budapest, The Hague, Hong Kong, London, New York, Paris, Shanghai, Vienna, and Washington, D.C. Two editions of the Barcelona Alumni Global Summit (2018 and 2019) have also been held. The Global Summit brings together Barcelona alumni, public authorities, and senior staff from local universities, research centers, and industry. Success so far entails building a dynamic and committed Barcelona Alumni Network that shares the vision of making Barcelona a key player in the scientific and technological global landscape while promoting responsible research and innovation among international alumni.

SciTech DiploHub has built an ecosystem that creates ample opportunities not only for Barcelona's universities to connect with their alumni abroad but also for the alumni themselves to connect with other scientists, researchers, and innovators while giving back to their cities, alma maters, and professional sectors. Although unique in their own ways, the Netherlands and Barcelona are not alone in mobilizing international alumni networks to spark innovation and regional reputation. Other countries have followed suit, such as Australia with its global alumni strategy to showcase itself as a contemporary, innovative, and open society (Australia Global Alumni 2016, 3). Higher education institutions in Denmark, France, Germany, Hungary, Sweden, and the United Kingdom are also reaping the benefits of connecting with their international alumni through country-sponsored alumni networks, organized and managed by national agencies to promote a country's public diplomacy, higher education, and trade. These types of international alumni networks include international graduates, or expat alumni, from any of the country's higher education institutions. They invest in international alumni networks primarily to brand their higher education institutions abroad, attract and retain international talent, and connect to public and private sectors abroad (Rincón and Rukowski 2015). Examples of national or city-led international alumni networks show that engaging international alumni can nurture their goodwill and loyalty to advance triangular collaborations with governments and industries and stimulate innovations and sustainable development.

International Alumni Embracing Social Responsibility

As universities focus their missions on educating global citizens, internationalization can contribute to socially embedded universities and civic engagement. According to Bawa and Munck (2012, xvi), a socially embedded university

> is—or should be—firmly committed to social transformation and the pursuit of knowledge for the benefit of the community. A socially embedded university becomes anchored in a community, with its positive democratic and communal values. In its turn, the university can (and does in part) put its considerable intellectual resources to imaginative use.

Global citizenship is inherent to socially embedded universities and civic engagement. In defining global citizen, Schattle (2008) identifies three primary, overlapping concepts: responsibility, awareness, and engagement. Similarly, Lilley, Barker, and Harris (2017) conceptualize a multilayered definition of the "ideal global graduate" as a critical and ethical global citizen underpinned by moral and transformative cosmopolitanism. Kahn and Agnew (2017) propose fostering global graduates through teaching diversity, critical self-reflection, self- and collective responsibility, and the ability to take action.

Global citizenship and civic engagement are essential to helping societies address pressing global challenges, as exemplified by the United Nations SDGs. Described in the 2030 Agenda for Sustainable Development, the SDGs are inspirational guides to ending poverty and bringing economic prosperity, social inclusion, environmental sustainability, peace, and good governance to all countries and people by 2030 (UN 2015). Universities, by creating and disseminating knowledge and educating global citizens, have a unique position within society, and therefore a critical role to play in achieving the SDGs. Engaging with the SDGs will greatly benefit universities by helping them demonstrate their social responsibility and positive global impact. Many universities are committing to include SDGs in education. In 2020, the Times Higher Education (THE) Impact Ranking assessed 766 universities across 85 countries and regions against the 17 SDGs. The ranking's main goal is to showcase universities that demonstrate commitment to making a positive social and economic impact: "At THE, we believe that universities represent the greatest hope of solving some of the world's biggest challenges" (THE 2020).

Many universities have started to engage their alumni locally and abroad to help embrace the SDGs. The 2020 THE Impact Ranking lists the University of Manchester as the top higher education institution in the United Kingdom—and in the top eight globally—for its social and environmental impact. Furthermore, the University of Manchester has the largest international alumni community of any campus-based university in the United Kingdom, with as many as 500,000 alumni in more than 190 countries.

A global finalist for the CASE Platinum Awards in 2020, selected as the best entry from Europe in the category "Best Practices in Alumni Relations," the University of Manchester is an inspiration for how higher education can play a key role in civic engagement and empower alumni to be socially responsible global citizens.

Chapter 6

CASE STUDY
Engaging International Alumni as Volunteers: Manchester Day of Action
By Markus Karlsson-Jones

Institution	University of Manchester
Motto	*Cognitio, sapientia, humanitas* (Knowledge, wisdom, humanity)
Founded	1824
Location	Manchester, United Kingdom
Number of Students in 2020	40,250 (29% of which are international)
Number of Alumni in 2020	508,561 (26% of which are international)
Department Responsible for International Alumni Relations	Division of Development and Alumni Relations
Alumni Relations Office Website	https://your.manchester.ac.uk/

Manchester Day of Action is a global volunteer activism program that inspires alumni worldwide to join together and support a local cause. In 2019, 380 alumni abroad organized 23 projects across 19 locations, accruing 1,300 hours of volunteering. These projects included cleaning beaches in Mumbai and San Francisco, gathering and distributing children's books for a pediatric ward in São Paulo, and hosting a sports day in Shanghai with people who have hearing and sight impairments. These projects all aligned with the aims of the SDGs and contributed to the university's Social Responsibility Agenda. It is one of the reasons why the university's societal impact has been ranked the top in the United Kingdom and eighth in the world by the THE University Impact Rankings in 2020. The program's name took inspiration from the civic celebration Manchester Day led by Manchester City Council in June each year. In June 2018, alumni were invited to celebrate their connections to Manchester by hosting their own local Manchester Day celebrations. This exercise, designed purely for engagement purposes initially, laid the blueprints for the volunteer activism program that Manchester Day of Action has become.

Audience

The program is geared to all 500,000 alumni worldwide. The primary focus is on the 26 percent of alumni who reside outside the United Kingdom, where opportunities for alumni to support the university's Social Responsibility Agenda are more limited.

Aims

The primary aim of this campaign is to engage alumni abroad, connecting alumni with each other and with the university. A closely related aim is to raise the profile of the university's Social Responsibility Agenda with international alumni by inspiring them to directly contribute. The program combines three powerful drivers:
1. Pride felt by alumni for their alma mater
2. Experiential engagement that gathers alumni around a common purpose
3. Cooperative community action and the desire to give back to a worthy cause

The motivator of this project, beyond the university's commitment to positive societal impact, is addressing the SDGs. The SDGs form the framework of the university's Social Responsibility Agenda; each Manchester Day of Action addresses one or more SDGs.

Other benefits include the following:
1. **Streamlined efforts:** Connect messaging with other Division of Development and Alumni Relations (DDAR) priorities (e.g., regular giving to raise the profile of the university's philanthropic causes).
2. **Reputation:** Enhance the university's reputation by internally and externally reporting on the combined effort of its international alumni community, telling a compelling story about the socially responsible impact of the global alumni network.
3. **Target markets:** Invite prospective students living in locations where recruitment is a priority to participate, thereby resonating with the social and ethical priorities the students share with the institution.

Responsibilities

The University of Manchester invites international alumni volunteers who run alumni groups abroad to help identify suitable local projects and convene a team of alumni to support them. This is an opportunity for local alumni to give hands-on support as a team. DDAR promotes this opportunity to alumni to get a team of volunteers together. Logistics are coordinated with charity and nonprofit organizations as needed. DDAR provides branded apparel (e.g., t-shirts, badges), allowing alumni to demonstrate their affiliation to the university. Volunteer organizers capture videos and images to tell the story afterward through the university's communication channels. DDAR captures and reports metrics on numbers of projects (including with which SDGs they align), numbers of volunteer participants, and the number of volunteering hours accrued.

Results

Every continent except Oceania took part in Manchester Day of Action in 2019. As previously noted, there were 23 projects in total, with 380 alumni participating, generating a total of 1,300 volunteer hours. Participants included a variety of international alumni groups—large and small, newly formed and well-established. All of the University of Manchester Worldwide Centers (Dubai, Hong Kong, Shanghai, and Singapore) helped to organize projects in partnership with international alumni volunteers.

The pilot event clearly indicated a strong appetite among international alumni to gather and volunteer their time for social, environmental, and community action. The alumni reported pride in playing an active role in the university's Social Responsibility Agenda. For example, Shahab Paracha, the secretary of the Alumni Association for Malaysia, led a project in Kuala Lumpur, convening a group of local graduates to work with children at an orphanage to discuss their career aspirations. Paracha says, "I'm a strong believer in inclusivity, and I feel that having alumni openly engaging with children from less fortunate backgrounds left a lasting impression, which ultimately inspired those children to do better in their studies and to be excited for their future."

Conclusion

Universities can help shape a positive future by educating global citizens and producing responsible research and innovation. International alumni networks provide universities and governments with a wealth of resourceful global citizens who can mobilize ideas, businesses, and people to create a more humane world. As Klaus Schwab (2015) writes:

> The Fourth Industrial Revolution may indeed have the potential to "robotize" humanity and thus to deprive us of our heart and soul. But as a complement to the best parts of human nature—creativity, empathy,

stewardship—it can also lift humanity into a new collective and moral consciousness based on a shared sense of destiny.

With their service missions, universities have the responsibility of envisioning a brighter future with students, academics, alumni, and society. Universities should keep nurturing global citizens with creativity, empathy, and stewardship to become responsible actors solving global challenges. International alumni networks are their loyal allies in the quest for a more peaceful and innovative world.

References

Advisory Council for Science, Technology and Innovation (AWTI). 2017. *STI Diplomacy: Advancing the Internationalisation of Science, Technology and Innovation.* The Hague: AWTI. https://www.awti.nl/documenten/adviezen/2017/05/16/vertaling-sti-diplomacy.

Australia Global Alumni. 2016. *Australia Global Alumni Engagement Strategy 2016–2020.* https://www.dfat.gov.au/sites/default/files/australia-global-alumni-engagement-strategy-2016-2020.pdf.

Bawa, Ahmed C., and Ronaldo Munck. 2012. "Foreword: Globalizing Civic Engagement." In *Higher Education and Civic Engagement: Comparative Perspectives,* eds. Lorraine McIlrath, Ann Lyons, and Ronaldo Munck. New York, NY: Palgrave MacMillan.

Dutta, Soumitra, Bruno Lanvin, and Sacha Wunsch-Vincent, eds. 2020. "Global Innovation Index (GII) 2020: Who Will Finance Innovation?" Thirteenth Edition. Cornell University, INSEAD, and the World Intellectual Property Organization. https://www.globalinnovationindex.org/Home.

Edison, Henry, Nauman bin Ali, and Richard Torkar. 2013. "Towards Innovation Measurement in the Software Industry." *Journal of Systems and Software* 86, 5:1390–407.

Eisenberg, Jaci, David Gann, and Saemoon Yoon. 2019. "How to Build an Entrepreneurial University." *World Economic Forum.* September 13. https://www.weforum.org/agenda/2019/09/how-to-build-an-entrepreneurial-university/.

European University Association (EUA). 2018. *The Future of Innovation Ecosystems: Recommendations from the European Smart Specialisation Workshop.* https://eua.eu/downloads/publications/the%20future%20of%20innovation%20ecosystems.pdf.

Gabriel, Mariya. 2020. "Insights from Commissioner Mariya Gabriel 'Towards Science Diplomacy in the European Union.'" *Science Diplomacy.* October 29.

https://www.science-diplomacy.eu/insights-from-commissioner-mariya-gabriel-towards-science-diplomacy-in-the-european-union/.

Global Innovation Index (GII). 2020. "Switzerland." *Global Innovation Index 2020.* https://www.wipo.int/edocs/pubdocs/en/wipo_pub_gii_2020/ch.pdf.

Howaldt, Jürgen, and Michael Schwarz. 2010. *Social Innovation: Concepts, Research Fields and International Trends, Volume 5.* Germany: RWTH Aachen University. http://www.sfs.tu-dortmund.de/cms/en/social_innovation/publications/IMO-MAG_Howaldt_final_mit_cover.pdf.

Kahn, Hilary, and Melanie Agnew. 2017. "Global Learning through Differences: Considerations for Teaching, Learning, and the Internationalization of Higher Education." *Journal of Studies in International Education* 21, 1:52–64.

Kardos, Mihaela. 2012. "The Relationship Between Entrepreneurship, Innovation and Sustainable Development. Research on European Union Countries." *Procedia Economics and Finance* 3:1030–5.

Knight, Jane. 2018. *Knowledge Diplomacy: A Bridge Linking International Higher Education and Research with International Relations.* British Council. https://www.britishcouncil.org/sites/default/files/kno.pdf.

Kreutz, Christian. 2016. "20+ Inspiring Social Innovation Lab Examples Worldwide." *Crisscrossed.* March 30. https://www.crisscrossed.net/2016/03/30/social-innovation-labs-worldwide/.

Lackéus, Martin. 2015. *Entrepreneurship in Education: What, Why, When, How.* https://www.oecd.org/cfe/leed/BGP_Entrepreneurship-in-Education.pdf/.

Lilley, Kathleen, Michelle Barker, and Neil Harris. 2017. "The Global Citizen Conceptualized: Accommodating Ambiguity." *Journal of Studies in International Education* 21, 1:6–21.

Nuffic. 2018. *A National Alumni Strategy.* https://www.nuffic.nl/sites/default/files/2020-08/a-national-alumni-strategy.pdf.

Organisation for Economic Co-operation and Development (OECD). 2005. *The Measurement of Scientific and Technological Activities: Oslo Manual. Guidelines for Collecting and Interpreting Technological Innovation Data, Third Edition.* Paris, France: OECD. https://ec.europa.eu/eurostat/ramon/statmanuals/files/9205111E.pdf.

Organisation for Economic Co-operation and Development (OECD). 2015. *The Innovation Imperative: Contributing to Productivity, Growth and Well-being.* Paris,

France: OECD Publishing. https://read.oecd-ilibrary.org/science-and-technology/the-innovation-imperative_9789264239814-en#page1.

Rincón, Sandra. 2018. "It's a Small World." *CASE Currents*. July/August:33–7. https://www.case.org/trending/issues/july-august-2018/its-small-world.

Rincón, Sandra, and Anne-Françoise Rutkowski. 2015. "The National Agenda and International Alumni Relations: Strategies of Engagement for the Future of European Higher Education." In *Staying Global: How International Alumni Relations Advances the Agenda*, ed. Gretchen Dobson. EAIE Occasional Paper 24.

Rogers, Everett M. 2003. *Diffusion of Innovations, Fifth Edition*. New York, NY: The Free Press.

Royal Society. 2010. *New Frontiers in Science Diplomacy*. London, UK: Royal Society. https://royalsociety.org/~/media/Royal_Society_Content/policy/publications/2010/4294969468.pdf.

Schattle, Hans. 2008. *The Practices of Global Citizenship*. Lanham, MD: Rowman & Littlefield.

Schwab, Klaus. 2015. "The Fourth Industrial Revolution: What It Means and How to Respond." *Foreign Affairs*. December 12. https://www.foreignaffairs.com/articles/2015-12-12/fourth-industrial-revolution.

Times Higher Education (THE). 2020. "Impact Rankings 2020." https://www.timeshighereducation.com/rankings/impact/2020/overall#!/page/0/length/25/sort_by/rank/sort_order/asc/cols/undefined.

United Nations (UN). 2015. *Transforming Our World: The 2030 Agenda for Sustainable Development*. https://sustainabledevelopment.un.org/content/documents/21252030%20Agenda%20for%20Sustainable%20Development%20web.pdf.

Urama, Kevin Chika, and Ernest Nti Acheampong. 2013. "Social Innovation Creates Prosperous Societies." *Stanford Social Innovation Review*, Summer. https://ssir.org/articles/entry/social_innovation_creates_prosperous_societies#:~:text=The%20old%20paradigm%20of%20government%20aid%20is%20inadequate.&text=What%20we%20need%20instead%20are,jobs%2C%20and%20increasing%20competitive%20abilities.

World Economic Forum. 2015. *Leveraging Entrepreneurial Ambition and Innovation: A Global Perspective on Entrepreneurship, Competitiveness and Development*. http://www3.weforum.org/docs/WEFUSA_EntrepreneurialInnovation_Report.pdf.

Conclusion: A World of Help

As exemplified in the preceding chapters, international alumni, with their professional expertise and diverse cultural backgrounds, can partner with their alma maters to cocreate new forms of engagement and solutions to local and global challenges. International alumni serve a variety of roles, and the impact of the efforts institutions and organizations take to develop a strong rapport with international alumni may be realized across their life cycle, starting as early as their student years. International alumni programs managed by dedicated staff and resourced effectively to support international alumni chapter networks, ambassador programs, and leadership training can best meet internationalization priorities now and in the future. Synthesizing key points presented throughout this book, this final chapter highlights two trends we predict will prevail in the future of international alumni relations: (1) virtual engagement and (2) national and transnational alumni networks.

International Alumni Engagement in the Twenty-First Century

Up until early 2020, many universities engaged international alumni with a few in-person events per year, organized to connect with visiting institutional delegates and peers from international alumni clubs, chapters, or associations. Social media use was encouraged as a tool to engage alumni abroad, but virtual alumni programming was a rarity. Now, as more universities offer their educational programs online and alumni relations offices provide online events, more virtual alumni programming can be envisioned to connect and engage alumni regardless of their place of residence. A prevalent component in many of the preceding case studies, online platforms have quickly evolved to facilitate digital alumni programming, such as online courses, lectures, webinars with breakout spaces for discussion, networking sessions, informal coffee breaks, and graduation ceremonies with their accompanying party celebrations. Universities and associations that now offer virtual alumni programming have seen a rapid increase of participating international alumni, compared to the number of participants who had attended in-person events. The different formats of virtual alumni programming allow universities to serve alumni at a scale that was not financially or logistically feasible before.

In addition, as regulations on individuals' privacy evolve to better protect personal data, universities will have to decide whether or not to solely depend on free social networks (e.g., Facebook and LinkedIn) that collect and own the alumni data. Digital alumni platforms have evolved to offer alternatives for universities to create international alumni communities, own the content collected, and have more control over who can view and use their alumni data. One of the main challenges for institutions that take this route will be to bring international alumni over to a new platform and create valuable, engaging content that will keep alumni coming back for more.

In the long-term, digital alumni programming can complement in-person international alumni engagement. Thus, the future of international alumni engagement might hold a combination of in-person events to socialize and celebrate with peers and university delegates, while digital activities focus on the personalized needs and preferences of alumni groups located locally and globally.

Global Alumni Networks to Meet Global Challenges

To maintain their country's innovation ecosystem, universities must keep educating and training talent on twenty-first century skills (e.g., entrepreneurship, technology, adaptability, global mindset, and social responsibility), generate new research, identify business opportunities, and grow multidisciplinary networks. International higher education contributes to social innovation through its international alumni as global citizens who can generate new ideas that meet local social needs, create multicultural relationships, and form new collaborations between civil society and their alma mater. International alumni networks, as social innovators, can help create triangular cooperation with start-ups, established companies, and academic research as well as build trust and strong collaboration with the public and private sectors. Thus, international alumni can support a university's service mission and social impact.

National or other large-scale alumni networks have been a growing trend with the goal of supporting social innovation locally and globally. In recent years, many European nations have been investing in establishing country- or city-wide alumni networks (e.g., NL alumni network or Barcelona Alumni). Other countries (e.g., Australia, Denmark, Germany, Hungary, Sweden, Taiwan, and the United Kingdom) have also joined this growing trend of developing their own global alumni networks. These global alumni networks aim to promote their country's public diplomacy and higher education institutions, attract and retain international talent, and foment trade and knowledge exchange. One of the latest developments that moves beyond the country level is EU ALUMNI. With the motto of "Engage locally, exchange globally," it is an umbrella network of former beneficiaries of EU-funded programs (e.g., Erasmus+, the Jean Monnet Programme, Marie Skłodowska-Curie Actions). This initiative advances the European Union's public diplomacy by creating common ground to cooperate locally for worldwide peace, security, and prosperity. Its multi-stakeholder approach aims to connect and strengthen the engagement between the European Union and international alumni, create one large international alumni community worldwide, and at the same time foster their engagement locally. It is possible the international alumni relations sector will see more regional alumni networks in the years to come.

These global alumni initiatives, whether at the city, country, or multinational levels, provide platforms where international alumni share an affinity not only with their alma mater but also with their host region. Global alumni networks can be vehicles to generate innovative solutions to global challenges.

International Alumni as Strategic Partners in Global Challenges and Beyond

To meet the current moment and find prompt solutions to global problems, international alumni engagement requires expertise, flexibility, and resources to quickly adapt to an uncertain future. Research demands international collaboration to find sustainable solutions to the many global challenges (e.g., climate change, escalating poverty, and health crises). International alumni can be strategic partners in finding short-term and long-term solutions to unprecedented challenges. Given that international alumni know their alma maters well, they can build common ground, generate knowledge to innovate, draw from real-life experiences, and contribute financial resources—all in service to the institution and its internationalization strategies. Their outstanding ability to meet the needs of their alma maters and other communities exemplifies how international alumni can be a world of help.

About the Authors and Contributors

Gretchen Dobson, EdD, is a global engagement specialist, author, and academic with more than 25 years of experience. She advises institutions, companies, organizations, and governments on creating sustainable strategies and solutions to best manage relationships with their global stakeholders and brand ambassadors.

Dobson is the author of *Being Global: Making the Case for International Alumni Relations* (CASE Books, 2011) and *the International Travel Handbook* (Academic Impressions, 2014) and editor of *Staying Global: How International Alumni Relations Advances the Agenda* (EAIE, 2015).

Dobson received her bachelor's and master's degrees from Boston College and a doctorate from the University of Pennsylvania. She holds faculty appointments with University at Albany in New York and Endicott College in Massachusetts. She is based in New South Wales, Australia.

Sandra Rincón, MSc, is founder and president of NL alumni network-Netherlands, senior consultant to EU ALUMNI, cofounder of Here2Start and Here2Work, and a PhD candidate at Tilburg University in the Netherlands. Her area of study is international alumni relations and international higher education.

With 30 years of experience in international education and intercultural communication, Rincón advises, trains, and coaches professionals on international engagement. She volunteers with the Council for Advancement and Support of Education (CASE), the European Association for International Education (EAIE), ICARe Alumni, and NAFSA: Association of International Educators and hosts *Brite Ideas*, a podcast for advancement professionals.

Rincón is an alum of the University of California-Davis, University of California-Irvine, and California State University-Fullerton. She has lived, studied, and worked in Colombia, the Netherlands, Spain, and the United States.

Contributors

Juan Maldonado Alcazar, MBA, is corporate and alumni relations manager at the Rotterdam School of Management (RSM), Erasmus University. He holds a BA from Universidad Iberoamericana and an MBA from RSM, where he applied his 10 years of customer journey experience to provide a new twist to alumni engagement. This has led him to win a CASE Circle of Excellence Award for his work revitalizing one of the largest and most successful mentoring programs in Europe, RSM MentorMe.

Andy Coxall, MA, chief executive of Common Purpose Student Experiences Limited, has more than 13 years of experience in the leadership development sector. He is a fellow of the Royal Society for the Encouragement of Arts, Manufactures, and Commerce (RSA). Coxall mentored for Chance UK, a charity that runs early intervention programs for children with behavioral difficulties, and volunteered with a street children program in Peru. Andy has an MA from the University of Edinburgh.

Huw Davies, Study UK Alumni campaign manager at the British Council, is responsible for delivering the global Study UK Alumni Awards. With more than 6 years of experience in internationalization of higher education, Davies is passionate about engaging international alumni, hearing their stories, and working with universities to share them. He received a BA degree from Swansea University.

Kathy Edersheim, MBA, has worked in alumni relations for more than 20 years, including founding the Yale Global Alumni Leadership Exchange and serving as part of the Yale Alumni Association management team. She advises and writes extensively on best practices in alumni relations, the power of community, and community management. Edersheim received a BA from Yale and an MBA from the Stern School of Business at New York University.

Kevin Fleming, PhD, is the cofounder and CEO of Prosper Nonprofit Advisors (www.prospernonprofits.com), a consultancy that helps nonprofit organizations achieve their philanthropy and engagement goals. He has more than 20 years of expertise in alumni engagement and nonprofit management through experiences at Mount Holyoke College, Emerson College, the University of Massachusetts-Amherst, Bowling Green State University, the University of Connecticut, and James Madison University. An educator, researcher, and thought leader, Fleming recently published a groundbreaking theory of alumni engagement in the peer-reviewed

Journal of Philanthropy & Education in an article titled "The Pots of Water Framework for Alumni Engagement." Fleming is an alum of James Madison University, Bowling Green State University, and the University of Massachusetts-Amherst.

Maria Gallo, EdD, is the founder and managing director of Keep in Touch Education (www.keepintoucheducation.com). She has more than 20 years of experience in leadership roles in higher education, including at the University of Toronto, University College Dublin, and the National University of Ireland-Galway. Gallo is also a visiting research fellow with the Trinity Business School, Trinity College Dublin, and the expert alumni adviser to the CERN Alumni Board. As a culmination of a decade of research in alumni engagement, she is publishing her first book, *The Alumni Way: Building Lifelong Value from Your University Investment* (Bristol University Press) in September 2021. Gallo is an alum of the University of Toronto (HBA in political science and criminology), University of Victoria (diploma in public sector management), University College Dublin (MA in public administration), University of Sheffield (EdD in higher education), and the National University of Ireland-Galway (certification in teaching and learning in higher education).

Jean Hamon, MBA, is the founder and CEO of Hivebrite, a comprehensive alumni engagement platform. Hivebrite empowers advancement professionals to create value and drive engagement at every step of the alumni journey. Hamon received an engineering degree from ESIEE Paris and an MBA from INSEAD.

Christie Johnson is the manager of international recruitment and partnerships within the Enrolment Services Department of Wilfrid Laurier University, her alma mater, for which she has worked since 2010. She is passionate about her role in creating and maintaining relationships on multiple levels: within and outside the university, with prospective and current students, with partners and educators, and of course with alumni. She has also earned professional certificates from the University of Manitoba and the University of Waterloo.

Markus Karlsson-Jones is senior alumni officer (global volunteer and networks) at the University of Manchester. Karlsson-Jones is responsible for programs to engage Manchester's global alumni network and activate the volunteers within it. Karlsson-Jones has 10 years of alumni relations experience, 6 of those specializing in international alumni relations. He helps export the city's phenomenal contributions to world culture. Karlsson-Jones received a BA in philosophy and international history from the University of Keele.

Jacqueline Kassteen has 20 years of international marketing experience in education, student travel, publishing, lead generation, retail, and financial services. She gives masterclasses and plenaries around the world and works as a consultant and project manager on branding, marketing techniques, recruitment and retention strategies, social media, alumni, product development, analysis, and research. Kassteen graduated from Rutgers University's School of Business and Douglass College.

Mariella Olivos, PhD, holds a doctorate from Tilburg University in the Netherlands, is the associate director of the bachelor programs at Universidad ESAN in Lima, Peru, and manages the institution's International Office. She is executive coordinator of the Latin American Council of Management Schools (CLADEA). Her research interest is in the area of internationalization strategies in higher education, entrepreneurship, global education, virtual teams, and cross-cultural studies.

Alexis Roig, MSc, serves as CEO of SciTech DiploHub, the Barcelona Science and Technology Diplomacy Hub. He is also a professor at the University of Shanghai for Science and Technology, associate researcher at the Barcelona Centre for International Relations, and associate professor of the Barcelona Institute of International Studies, and he has more than 10 years of experience as a senior adviser in science diplomacy for governments across Asia, Europe, and Latin America. Roig has an MSc in computer science from Universitat Politècnica de Catalunya, a master's in business administration and entrepreneurship from EM Normandie International Business School, and a postgraduate diploma in diplomatic practices from the United Nations Institute for Training and Research.

Brittany Russell, MEd, a two-time alum of Wilfrid Laurier University, holds the role of alumni relations officer of chapters and regional programming at her alma mater. She works to keep alumni connected to their alma mater through events that support both personal and professional development growth with the intention to provide outlets and resources for inspiring lives of leadership and purpose.

Alyssa Shoup, EdD, is a higher education professional focused on impactful and transformational international alumni and constituent engagement. Earning her bachelor's and master's degrees and doctorate from the University of Rochester, she is a proud lifelong Rochesterian and Yellowjacket.

Mark C. Sollis is known globally for his cutting-edge and disruptive thinking in alumni engagement. He specializes in strategy and planning, business performance and metrics, and digital and interest-based engagement. Sollis is a proud an active alum of Mount Royal University.

Serge Sych, EdD, is vice president for enrollment management, career services, and alumni relations at Central European University (Austria and Hungary). He is an award-winning higher education leader, frequent international speaker, senior faculty trainer, and member of the volunteer leadership bodies of CASE Europe and the European Association for International Education. Sych has earned the following degrees: EdD in education, University College London's Institute of Education; LLM in comparative constitutional law, Central European University; MA in international relations and European studies, the Open University; and MA in history and political science, Donetsk National University.

Martine Torfs, MA, head of the Alumni Team at the KU Leuven Fundraising and Alumni Relations Office, is responsible for engaging the university's worldwide alumni network. With more than 20 years of experience in internationalization of higher education, she is passionate about aligning alumni programs and internationalization strategies with the goal of creating a dynamic international stakeholder community for the university. She has a background in Chinese studies and intercultural relations and is an enthusiastic alum of KU Leuven, Universidad de Salamanca, Xiamen University, and Beijing Foreign Studies University.

Şule Yalçın, MSc, career development and alumni relations manager at Sabancı University, coordinates projects targeting employability of undergraduate students and alumni activities. With around 20 years of experience in higher education, she works as the talent acquisition executive, building strategic alumni networks and engagements across the world. She holds BSc and MSc degrees in horticultural crops from Ankara University and Cukurova University respectively, and is currently pursuing a PhD in business administration at Istanbul Arel University.

A Note on Process

Writing *Engaging International Alumni as Strategic Partners* has been a truly collaborative experience that has allowed us to learn from each other and colleagues around the world while continuing to develop our expertise in the field.

For me (Sandra), my personal experience as an immigrant, international student, international alum, trained international educator, and researcher has guided me to create, lead, and execute institutional strategies on comprehensive internationalization. For the past 15 years, I have concentrated on creating and leading strategies for international alumni relations to advance internationalization at institutional and national levels. My two main research topics are (1) global competence and social responsibility and (2) international alumni networks as social innovators.

I (Gretchen) have focused the past 20 years of my professional career on building awareness of international alumni relations and the power of global networks—one graduate at a time. I have introduced the topic of global alumni relations to graduate education programs and am deepening my involvement in government-led development programs that are investing in their soft power diplomacy via international alumni capacity-building.

After working together on an outline that melded our respective expertise into a cohesive resource, we divided up the chapters based on our strengths. Sandra took the lead on chapters 1 through 3 and the sections in chapter 6 on (1) professional development and employability and (2) innovation and social responsibility. Gretchen steered chapter 4 and the chapter 6 section on (1) brand and reputational management and (2) attracting and recruiting talent. Though this project started as two authors with distinct backgrounds in the field coming together, the content has been strengthened by the two-way feedback along the way. We are grateful for this opportunity to apply our respective expertise to create a helpful resource for the field.

www.ingramcontent.com/pod-product-compliance
Lightning Source LLC
Chambersburg PA
CBHW061447300426
44114CB00014B/1870